Oxford English
Source Books

BOOK 1
**Here, Now
And Beyond**

BOOK 2
Truth To Tell

BOOK 3
Half-way

NANCY MARTIN

Truth To Tell

c

OXFORD UNIVERSITY PRESS

Oxford University Press, Ely House, London W 1

GLASGOW NEW YORK TORONTO MELBOURNE WELLINGTON
CAPE TOWN IBADAN NAIROBI DAR ES SALAAM LUSAKA ADDIS ABABA
DELHI BOMBAY CALCUTTA MADRAS KARACHI LAHORE DACCA
KUALA LUMPUR SINGAPORE HONG KONG TOKYO

First published 1968
Reprinted (with corrections) 1970, 1972

Filmset by St. Paul's Press Limited, Malta
and Printed in Great Britain by
Butler and Tanner Limited, Frome, Somerset

CONTENTS

reminiscence — fiction — legend

If you listen to the talk that goes on around you, you will find that most of it is made up of small stories. People like to tell what happen ...

Grown-ups exchange stories ...

... is a reminiscence, that is a remembering of things as they happened, so it is a true story. It was told by an old man called William Kemp to his son. William Kemp died in 1906 aged 91 and his son is now an old man, so the story goes back well over a hundred years but it is still within living memory.

Witches at Hallowe'en

I reckon I was a lad of about seven or eight when, because Mother was expecting another little one to join our already crowded house, I was sent to stay with an old aunt in one of the loneliest parts of the Fens. She had a big family, this aunt, though most of them were grown up by then, except for a boy of fifteen and a girl of twelve. Although there wasn't another house within a mile that didn't bother them; the farm was run by the family and for most of the year they went to bed when it got dark and got up at daybreak.

While I was there Hallowe'en came round. In the afternoon everyone was busy putting osier twigs in front of all the doors and windows, the pig-styes, stables and cowhouse. Uncle killed one of his black hens and hung it on the chicken house door after he'd pulled out two of its wing feathers and tied them on the yard dog's collar; then he caught the cats and shut them up in the barn. From all the talk going on I found out that this was the night when the witches went around the Fen meeting each other and then, at the chiming of midnight, coming to some spot they'd chosen and casting spells over all the folks and animals nearby. That was why the peeled osier rods were put at all the ways into the house because no witch dared cross over them, neither would they go near the black chicken feathers.

As the evening went by we all sat around the big open hearth. Aunt didn't put peat on the fire that night because witches could smell peat smoke for miles away, she said; instead, huge logs of oak were blazing away. The candles had been blown out so the only light we had came from the fire as we sat and listened to Aunt's stories of what witches could get up to. After supper a plate of thick slices of ham and half a loaf of bread were stood outside on the doorstone so that, if a witch called, she wouldn't have to go away hungry because, if she did, she might start casting spells on us. Then I was given a glass of ginger wine while my aunt and uncle and the others drank a lot of home-made botanic beer. After a while Uncle stood up and said to me:

'Come along, it's time we were up and doing.'

He told me it was the custom, this night, for the oldest man and the youngest boy in the house to go round the farm an hour before midnight; so we set off. It was very queer paddling along behind Uncle as he carried the lantern. All the animals seemed restless and Uncle said they were like that because they could see and hear things that we couldn't, and they all knew what was going on.

After we'd been round the farmyard we had to visit the bees. As we went into the orchard an owl swooped over us with a loud screech, just above Uncle's head. I was scared, but Uncle got a firm grip of the thick stick he was carrying and, when the owl turned to fly over us again, he caught it such a clout that it fell down to the ground, fluttered its wings a bit and then lay still. My uncle bent down, turned it over and said:

'Well, there's one old witch who won't go home tonight.'

When we got to the bee-hive we went close up and listened to the noise going on inside it; it was just like the hum of a threshing tackle on a frosty morning.

'Bor,' said Uncle, 'they're all worked up because they're a lot wiser than we are;' then, after tapping the hive with his stick, he bent right down to the entrance and said:

'Well done, my old beauties; I got one just now and, by the sound of it, you've got another; push her outside when you've done with her.'

When we were back indoors we all sat round the fire again while Uncle told my aunt and the others what had happened while we ...

'It looks as though ...

..., I promise I'll ... ...ght before she gets to the hearth. This ought to make her sneeze a bit first,' and she took a handful of flowers of sulphur out of the bag and threw them on the fire. Bright blue flames and yellow smoke roared up the chimney. Aunt did this several times although Uncle told her not to forget the roof was thatch and if we were burnt out it wasn't going to be any good blaming it on any witches; but she only told him to be quiet, she knew what she was doing. This started a lot of arguing, everybody joining in till it seemed to me that the witches had been forgotten and that I was in the middle of a good old family row. Anyway, Aunt got in such a temper that she threw the whole bag on the fire and the yellow smoke came pouring out into the room worse than ever, making us all splutter and choke.

Uncle said that two could play at that game and he went over to the cupboard and fetched out a linen bag full of the black gunpowder he used in his muzzle loader. He'd no sooner hurled it at the back of the fire than there was a hell of a bang and we were all smothered in soot from head to foot. Well, that cooled everybody's temper and when the smoke had cleared away a bit Uncle said:

'Well I'll be damned,' because lying on Auntie's lap was a jackdaw, just kicking out his last gasp. And just then the old grandfather clock struck midnight.

After that we all ate a lot of thick ham sandwiches and Uncle said to me:

'Come on Bor, we've got to make another round.'

It was still very dark when we got outside but all the animals were

¹'tudded' means toaded or bewitched.

quiet and settled down. When we got to the orchard we found the bees quiet too, but on the flight board, believe it or not, was a dead mouse, still warm. Uncle picked it up then went back to fetch the owl which he'd killed the time we were out before. When we were back in the house he threw the owl, the mouse and the jackdaw on the fire and said:

'Three witches on one Hallowe'en isn't a bad bag. Now, all of you get up to bed and sleep well, you won't have to worry about any witches for another twelvemonth.' WILLIAM KEMP

From *More Tales from the Fens* by W.H. BARRETT

For writing and discussion

Don t know *columns? Would your answer be true?*

Describe the 'setting' for a weird story; a story you half believe in. Write about the room or the place, the time of day, and who was there besides yourself. Try to write in such a way that no one wants to laugh, let alone dares to!

If you think you can carry it off write the story itself – but you ought to pay a forfeit if you make people laugh.

Write or discuss some common superstitions – would you confess to believing in any yourself?

Write a story about a twentieth-century witch in England. This might be funny or serious.

No one actually sees any witches in William Kemp's story, though everyone was convinced they would be about the farm house on Hallowe'en in some disguise or other. What do you think about the events described?

Here is another reminiscence. It is by a retired smuggler from Devonshire and was written more than twenty years after his smuggling days were over when he had become respectable and law-abiding. You may find the language difficult at first because he lived over a hundred and fifty years ago. England was then at war with the French under Napoleon.

From *The Memoirs of John Rattenbury, Smuggler, of Beer, Devonshire. 1837*

I now seriously resolved to abandon my trade of smuggling; to take a public house, and to employ my leisure hours in fishing etc. At first the house appeared to answer pretty well, but after being in it for two years, I found that I was considerably gone back in the world; and that my circumstances, instead of improving, were daily getting worse, for all the money I could get by fishing and piloting, went to the brewer, with whom the business was confined; and the times were very hard, trade and commerce being in a state of great stagnation. Thus situated and not knowing what else to do, I now returned to my old trade of smuggling, and in November, 1812, went in a vessel to Alderney, but returning home, about the middle of the channel, at day-break we fell in with one of his majesty's cruisers, which afterwards proved to be the Catherine brig, commanded by Captain Tingle. A very warm chase then ensued, in the course of which, she fired twenty-four cannon-shot at us; in consequence of which we were thrown into the greatest alarm, not knowing whether we had fallen in with a French privateer, or an English vessel. About half-past ten o'clock in the morning they came so near to us, that finding that there was no hope of escaping, we hauled down all our sails. The crew, however, still kept up an incessant fire of small arms upon us, several of which went through our binnacle and bulwarks, and the sails we had hauled down. All the men except myself were below, and in the midst of this tremendous volley, I escaped without a single wound; a circumstance on which I have since reflected not without wonder; but my mind was then in such a state of excitement, that I thought but little of the danger to which I was exposed.

When the captain came within hail of us, he called out, 'You rascals, I will put you all on board a man-of-war.'[1] To his great disappointment, however, upon inspecting our vessel he found nothing on board her, except a pint of gin in a bottle; but he detained the vessel; and having put myself and my companions on board his own brig, took us into Brixham. The same day I asked the captain to grant me leave to go on

[1] Having to serve on a man-of-war was often thought worse than going to prison.

shore, which he peremptorily refused; and when he went off in a boat himself, he gave the men a very particular ch~~~~ ~~~~ ~

~~~~~ ~ ~~~~~~~~ ~~~~~~~~~~~~

~~~~~, unless I receive orders to that effect from the Board.' The following day, the Catherine brig being convoy to the Brixham fishermen, he went to sea, and took us cruising with him for about a week. When we came into the bay again, I once more reiterated my request, but with no better success; and, as he stepped over the side of the vessel to go on shore, he told the crew to keep a sharp look-out for if they suffered one of us to escape, one of them should suffer in his stead. The same day, my wife, having heard of my situation, with some other females, the wives of my companions, came on board. Our interview was short; but long enough for me to entreat her to get a good boat, and come off to me the next morning. In the evening, I opened part of my plan to my companions; and desired them to be prepared to act according to the hints I had given them. When she came, which was about ten o'clock in the morning, the other officers being on shore, the second mate had the charge of the vessel, which was a circumstance favourable to my design. As soon as she and the other females were alongside, I jumped into the boat, and made a motion to my companions to do the same, that we might assist them on board; one of them did so, and I whispered to him to wait till they were all out of the boat; and, immediately upon this being accomplished, I called out loud, 'Shove off' upon which, three other of my companions jumped in. I then put my oar against the side of the vessel; but the second mate caught hold of it, and broke off the blade. Being very angry, I threw the remaining part at him, and called to my companions to hoist the sail. He exclaimed, 'If you do, I'll fire at you,' to which I replied, 'Make sure of your mark.' At this he fired, and the shot went

through the sails; he was preparing to do so again, when my wife wrested the piece out of his hands. Having recovered it, he fired ᵃᵍᵃⁱ shot striking the rope of the sail ᵢₜ fₐₗₗ thinking thᵃₜ

...ₒₛₑ ₜₒ my head,

... as I got on shore, I scrambled up the cliffs; and, when I reached the top, I looked back, but could see no one. I then took off my jacket, and left it behind me, thinking that if they met with it, they would suppose that I had thrown it off to facilitate my speed in getting away. After this, I rolled myself down the cliffs, not far from where we landed. At the same time, I saw our pursuers following my companions, and several hundred people on Brixham hills looking on; but they were too far off to give them the least assistance. It was now about eleven o'clock. I was without hat or jacket, and the rain descended in torrents. I found out the best retreat I could among the rocks, and remained there till four o'clock in the afternoon. About one, I saw the men belonging to the brig go by and embark; and when all seemed quiet I started over hedges, fields and ditches, and got to Torquay; and went to a public-house kept by a friend, where I got dry clothes and refreshments. I then sent a man and horse to my wife, and directed her to meet me on the next day. The following morning I received a letter informing me that two of my companions were retaken; and, when my wife arrived, she told me that they had both been sentenced to go on board a man-of-war bound for the West Indies. We then set off together, and got home safe to Beer.

The Thames sailing barge Venta. This boat is about 80 years old.

Fire Brig.   Flat Bottomed Boat.   Gun Vefsel *(the Wolverine.)*   Man of War's Long B

Engraving of British war ships, 1802.

For writing and discussion

Read this story carefully and discuss what happened.

There are some things you will need to find out from reference books, or
a teacher, such as:

What 'privateers' were.

How the British navy recruited its sailors by means of the 'Press Gang'
and what the Press Gang was.

Why ordinary men as well as law-breakers dreaded the Press Gang.

What things were highly taxed and therefore were smuggled into the
country.

How the Government attempted to stop this.

What kind of tricks the smugglers used to outwit the Customs officers
and the Royal Navy.

FICTION OR TRUE STORIES?

Some notes on how I hoodwinked the Customs

On one occasion I had ...

... which means I recovered the silks perfect and uninjured.

Having landed a cargo at Seaton Hole one dark night, I was going up the cliff with a keg at my back, when I had the ill-luck to stumble over an ass, which began to bray so horribly that together with the noise occasioned by my fall, woke an officer who was taking a nap below, in consequence of which he seized nearly forty kegs being the whole of the cargo.

One day hearing that my son, whom I had sent to Seaton with a flagon of brandy, had been taken by a Preventive man, I seized a poker and ran out to effect his rescue, but I found that he escaped observation through climbing up into a tree.

To these I might add many more of a similar nature.

1. *Write the story of John Rattenbury's adventure (on this occasion) in your own words. Use the first person ('I').*

2. *Write a story (fiction) about smuggling today.*

3. *Write about a chase in which you escaped (fiction or reminiscence).*

4. *Write a story in which you hide something in a special place (fiction or reminiscence). It may be quite a small or unimportant thing that you hide.*

5. *Wild creatures always hide from human beings. Imagine you are a fox or a hare or a squirrel or a mouse or any other creature running away and hiding. Write about how things looked to you, what happened, and how you felt.*

The Story-Teller

It was a hot afternoon, and the railway carriage was correspondingly sultry, and the next stop was at Templecombe, nearly an hour ahead. The occupants of the carriage were a small girl, and a smaller girl, and a small boy. An aunt belonging to the children occupied one corner seat, and the further corner seat on the opposite side was occupied by a bachelor who was a stranger to their party, but the small girls and the small boy emphatically occupied the compartment. Both the aunt and the children were conversational in a limited, persistent way, reminding one of a house-fly that refused to be discouraged. Most of the aunt's remarks seemed to begin with 'Don't', and nearly all of the children's remarks began with 'Why?' The bachelor said nothing out loud.

'Don't, Cyril, don't,' exclaimed the aunt, as the small boy began smacking the cushions of the seat, producing a cloud of dust at each blow.

'Come and look out of the window,' she added.

The child moved reluctantly to the window. 'Why are those sheep being driven out of that field?' he asked.

'I expect they are being driven to another field where there is more grass,' said the aunt weakly.

'But there is lots of grass in that field,' protested the boy, 'there's nothing else but grass there. Aunt, there's lots of grass in that field.'

'Perhaps the grass in the other field is better,' suggested the aunt fatuously.

'Why is it better?' came the swift, inevitable question.

'Oh, look at those cows!' exclaimed the aunt. Nearly every field along the line had contained cows or bullocks, but she spoke as if she were drawing attention to a rarity.

'Why is the grass in the other field better?' persisted Cyril.

The frown on the bachelor's face was deepening to a scowl. He was a hard, unsympathetic man, the aunt decided in her mind. She was utterly unable to come to any satisfactory decision about the grass in the other field.

The smaller girl created a diversion by beginning to recite 'On the Road to Mandalay.' She only knew the first line, but she put her limited knowledge to the fullest possible use. She repeated the line over and over again in a dreamy but resolute and very audible voice; it seemed to the bachelor that someone had had a bet with her that she

[text obscured]

[...] interrupted at frequent intervals by loud, petulant questions from her listeners, she began an unenterprising and deplorably uninteresting story about a little girl who was good, and made friends with everyone on account of her goodness, and was finally saved from a mad bull by a number of rescuers who admired her moral character.

'Wouldn't they have saved her if she hadn't been good?' demanded the bigger of the small girls. It was exactly the question that the bachelor had wanted to ask.

'Well, yes,' admitted the aunt lamely, 'but I don't think they would have run quite so fast to her help if they had not liked her so much.'

'It's the stupidest story I've ever heard,' said the bigger of the small girls, with immense conviction.

'I didn't listen after the first bit, it was so stupid,' said Cyril.

The smaller girl made no actual comment on the story, but she had long ago recommenced a murmured repetition of her favourite line.

'You don't seem to be a success as a story-teller,' said the bachelor suddenly from his corner.

The aunt bristled in instant defence at this unexpected attack.

'It's a very difficult thing to tell stories that children can both understand and appreciate,' she said stiffly.

'I don't agree with you,' said the bachelor.

'Perhaps *you* would like to tell them a story,' was the aunt's retort.

'Tell us a story,' demanded the bigger of the small girls.

'Once upon a time,' began the bachelor, 'there was a little girl called Bertha, who was extraordinarily good.'

The children's momentarily-aroused interest began to flicker; all stories seemed dreadfully alike, no matter who told them.

'She did all she was told, she was always truthful, she kept her clothes clean, ate milk puddings as though they were jam tarts, learned her lessons perfectly, and was polite in her manners.'

'Was she pretty?' asked the bigger of the small girls.

'Not as pretty as any of you,' said the bachelor, 'but she was horribly good.'

There was a wave of reaction in favour of the story; the word horrible in connection with goodness was a novelty that recommended itself. It seemed to introduce a ring of truth that was absent from the aunt's tales of infant life.

'She was so good,' continued the bachelor, 'that she won several medals for goodness, which she always wore, pinned on to her dress. There was a medal for obedience, another medal for punctuality, and a third for good behaviour. They were large metal medals and they clicked against one another as she walked. No other child in the town where she lived had as many as three medals, so everybody knew that she must be an extra good child.'

'Horribly good,' quoted Cyril.

'Everybody talked about her goodness, and the Prince of the country got to hear about it, and he said that as she was so very good she might be allowed once a week to walk in his park, which was just outside the town. It was a beautiful park, and no children were ever allowed in it, so it was a great honour for Bertha to be allowed to go there.'

'Were there any sheep in the park?' demanded Cyril.

'No,' said the bachelor, 'there were no sheep.'

'Why weren't there any sheep?' came the inevitable question arising out of that answer.

The aunt permitted herself a smile, which might almost have been described as a grin.

'There were no sheep in the park,' said the bachelor, 'because the Prince's mother had once had a dream that her son would either be killed by a sheep or else by a clock falling on him. For that reason the Prince never kept a sheep in his park or a clock in his palace.'

The aunt suppressed a gasp of admiration.
'Was the Prince killed by a ~~ch~~ ~~~~ ~~~~ ~~~~ ~~~~

~~~~~~~~~~~~~~~~~~~, then he resumed:

'Bertha was rather sorry to find that there were no flowers in the park. She had promised her aunts, with tears in her eyes, that she would not pick any of the kind Prince's flowers, and she had meant to keep her promise, so of course it made her feel silly to find that there were no flowers to pick.'

'Why weren't there any flowers?'

'Because the pigs had eaten them all,' said the bachelor promptly. 'The gardeners had told the Prince that you couldn't have pigs and flowers, so he decided to have pigs and no flowers.'

There was a murmur of approval at the excellence of the Prince's decision; so many people would have decided the other way.

'There were lots of other delightful things in the park. There were ponds with gold and blue and green fish in them, and trees with beautiful parrots that said clever things at a moment's notice, and humming birds that hummed all the popular tunes of the day. Bertha walked up and down and enjoyed herself immensely, and thought to herself: "If I were not so extraordinarily good I should not have been allowed to come into this beautiful park and enjoy all that there is to be seen in it," and her three medals clinked against one another as she walked and helped to remind her how very good she really was. Just then an enormous wolf came prowling into the park to see if he could catch a fat little pig for his supper.'

'What colour was it?' asked the children, amid an immediate quickening of interest.

'Mud-colour all over, with a black tongue and pale grey eyes that gleamed with unspeakable ferocity. The first thing that they saw in the park was Bertha; her pinafore was so spotlessly white and clean that it could be seen from a great distance. Bertha saw the wolf and saw that it was stealing towards her, and she began to wish that she had never been allowed to come into the park. She ran as hard as she could, and the wolf came after her with huge leaps and bounds. She managed to reach a shrubbery of myrtle bushes and she hid herself in one of the thickest of the bushes. The wolf came sniffing among the branches, its black tongue lolling out of its mouth and its pale grey eyes glaring with rage. Bertha was terribly frightened, and thought to herself: "If I had not been so extraordinarily good I should have been safe in the town at this moment." However, the scent of the myrtle was so strong that the wolf could not sniff out where Bertha was hiding and the bushes were so thick that he might have hunted about in them for a long time without catching sight of her, so he thought he might as well go off and catch a little pig instead. Bertha was trembling very much at having the wolf prowling and sniffing so near her, and as she trembled the medal for obedience clinked against the medals for good conduct and punctuality. The wolf was just moving away when he heard the sound of the medals clinking and stopped to listen; they clinked again in a bush quite near him. He dashed into the bush, his pale grey eyes gleaming with ferocity and triumph and dragged Bertha out and devoured her to the last morsel. All that was left of her were her shoes, bits of clothing, and the three medals for goodness.'

'Were any of the little pigs killed?'

'No, they all escaped.'

'The story began badly,' said the smaller of the small girls, 'but it had a beautiful ending.'

'It is the most beautiful story that I ever heard,' said the bigger of the small girls with immense decision.

'It is the *only* beautiful story I have ever heard,' said Cyril.

A dissentient opinion came from the aunt.

'A most improper story to tell to young children! You have undermined the effect of years of careful teaching.'

'At any rate,' said the bachelor, collecting his belongings preparatory to leaving the carriage, 'I kept them quiet for ten minutes which was more than you were able to do.'

(Warning! There are no right or wrong answers to these questions.)

What actually happens in this story?

Unlike the first two stories this one is about ordinary things—some bored children in a railway carriage being told a story to keep them quiet; it is called The Story-Teller *so we are probably invited by the author to regard it as fiction. Are there any parts of it that you think are true?*

Why do you think the Aunt thought it was an improper story to tell young children? The bachelor, judging by his last remarks, seems to agree with her. What do you think? Is it improper for you?

The story is about some small children, a couple of grown-ups, a wolf, a good little girl, little pigs, and a Prince. Is it, in fact, a children's story?

Would anyone be likely to say after this story, 'I don't believe it'?
What kind of stories do you like?
Why do you think the children liked the story?

Two children were talking about this story.
'Everyone in it is horrid,' said one.
'Not at all,' replied the other, 'everyone in it is funny.'
What do you think?

For writing

1. *Write a story about an occasion when a boy or girl was bad, and knew it. Write as though you were the boy or girl and use the first person ('I'). Describe your 'hero's' thoughts and feelings as well as what he did.*

2. *Write a poem about being angry.*

3. *Write a story of Red Riding Hood and the Wolf as the Bachelor might have told it, or in any other way that pleases you, and which is different from the way it appears in the children's story-books.*

4. *Write a story, as you would tell it, for some children of 5 or 6 or 7 years old. Think of any children of this age that you know, younger brothers or sisters or cousins for instance.*

5. *Write about a friend. How you first met him or her and what you do together; how you have quarrelled and made it up again, or perhaps drifted apart and found other friends.*

6. *Write a story about being lonely and trying to find a friend.*

7. *Write about why you would or would not like to be grown up.*

You may prefer to write poems instead of stories on any of the subjects suggested.

There is another kind of story which probably began by being true and which was preserved for hundreds of years by people telling it to each other before it was written down. Each teller changed it slightly and embroidered it to make it a better story (think of the fishing or golf stories that grown-ups tell) until in the end it became almost pure fiction.

People now think that the story of the voyage of the ship *Argo* and Jason's search for the Golden Fleece was really a gold raid. In Aeetes' kingdom on the Black Sea the rivers brought down gold dust which was caught in the wool of sheepskins placed in the rivers. So Jason's adventure was really a piratical adventure, and a princess who was also an heiress was just as valuable a prize as a fleece full of gold dust.

Though these may be the economic and historical facts behind the events, the story itself is concerned with people and how they felt and what they did.

...her father could not fail to know what she had done for Jason, and that she would soon be called on to pay the price in full. She also feared the maids who had seen something of their secret meeting. She cleared her lap of deadly drugs and poured them all back into their box. She kissed her bed; she kissed the posts on either side of the folding doors; she stroked the walls of her room. Then, tearing off one of her long tresses, she left it there for her mother in memory of her girlhood and said her sad goodbye:

'Mother, I go, leaving this lock here in my stead. Farewell; for I am going far away. Farewell my home and all it holds. Oh, Jason, you should never have come here! I wish the sea had been the end of you.'

With that she went. She ran barefoot down narrow alleys, holding her mantle over her forehead with her left hand to hide her face, and with the other lifting up the hem of her skirt. Swiftly and fearfully she passed across the great city by a secret way, and so beyond the walls, unrecognized by any of the watch, who had not even seen her in her flight, and presently, to her relief, found herself on the high bank of the river, and looking across it caught the gleam of a bonfire which the Argonauts kept blazing all night in celebration of their triumph. She sent a clear call ringing through the dark and Jason recognized her voice and told the rest, who were speechless with amazement when they realized the truth. Medea called three times; three times at the bidding of the others Jason shouted back, and all the while they were rowing eagerly towards her.

Even before they had made fast to the opposite bank, Jason leapt lightly to the ground from *Argo*'s deck. He was followed by Phrontis and Argus, and at once Medea's arms were round their knees and she was making her appeal: 'My dear ones, save me from Aeetes, save yourselves! All is discovered, all; and there is nothing we can do. Let us sail away before that man can even mount his chariot; and I myself will give you the golden fleece, putting the guardian snake to sleep.'

She spoke in anguish and fell at Jason's feet; but what she said had warmed his heart. At once he raised her tenderly and embraced her and, to comfort her, he said: 'Dear lady, I swear that when we are back in Hellas I will take you into my home as my own wedded wife.' And with that he took her right hand in his own.

They took her on board at once, thrust *Argo* from the bank, and rowed off, waking the night as they struck the water with their pine-wood blades. It was then that Medea had a wild moment of regret. She started to go back, stretching her hands out to the shore. But Jason went to her with reassuring words and checked her desperate design.

He and Medea reached their goal late at night. A path led them to the sacred wood, where they were making for the huge oak on which the fleece was hung, bright as a cloud incarnadined by the fiery beams of the rising sun. But the serpent with his sharp unsleeping eyes had seen them coming and now confronted them, stretching out his long neck and hissing terribly. The high banks of the river and the deep recesses of the wood threw back the sound, and far away babies sleeping in their mothers' arms were startled by the hiss, and their anxious mothers waking in alarm hugged them closer to their breasts.

The monster in his sheath of horny scales rolled forward his interminable coils, like the eddies of black smoke that spring from smouldering logs and chase each other from below in endless convolutions. But as he writhed he saw the maiden take her stand, and heard her in her sweet voice charming him to sleep. Jason from behind looked on in terror. But the giant snake, enchanted by her song, was soon relaxing the whole length of his serrated spine and smoothing out his multitudinous undulations, like a dark and silent swell rolling across a sluggish sea. Yet his grim head still hovered over them and the cruel jaws threatened to snap them up. But Medea, chanting a spell, dipped a fresh sprig of juniper in her brew and sprinkled his eyes with her most potent drug and as the all-pervading magic scent spread round his head, sleep fell on him.

Stirring no more, he let his jaw sink to the ground, and his innumerable

full moon as it climbs the sky and looks into her attic room. The ram's skin with its golden covering was as large as the hide of a yearling heifer or a brocket, as a young stag is called by hunting folk. The long flocks weighed it down and the very ground before him as he walked was bright with gold. When he slung it on his left shoulder, as he did at times, it reached his feet. But now and again he made a bundle of it in his arms. He was mortally afraid that some god or man might rob him on the way.

Dawn was spreading over the world when they rejoined the rest. The young men marvelled when they saw the mighty fleece, and they all leapt up in their eagerness to touch it and hold it in their hands. But Jason kept them off and threw a new mantle over the fleece. Then he led Medea aft, found her a seat, and addressed his men.

'My friends,' he said, 'let us start for home without delay. The prize for which we dared greatly and suffered misery on the cruel sea is ours. And the task proved easy, thanks to this lady, who I intend, with her consent, to bring home with me and wed. You too must cherish her: she is the true saviour of Achaea and yourselves.

I spoke of haste, for I am sure that Aeetes and his mob are on their way to bar our passage from the river to the sea. So man the ship, man every bench, two men on each, taking it in turns to row. That will leave half of you to hold aloft your ox-hide shields against the arrows of the enemy and protect us as we get away. Remember, we hold the future of our children, our dear country, and our aged parents in our hands.'

With that he donned his arms. The eager crew responded with a great shout, and Jason drawing his sword cut through the hawsers at the stern. Then, in his battle gear, he took his stand beside Medea and the steersman

Ancaeus; and *Argo* leapt forward to the oars as the crew strained every nerve to bring her clear of the river.

By now the haughty king and all his Colchians were well aware of Medea's love for Jason and the part she had played. In full armour they gathered in the market-place, countless as the waves of the sea whipped up by the winter storm. So in their multitudes they streamed along the banks of the river in full cry. Aeetes in his fine chariot, with its wind-swift horses stood out above them all. In his left hand he held a round shield, in the other a long torch of pinewood, and his huge spear lay beside him pointing to the front. Apsyrtus held the reins.

But the ship, swept down the broad stream by the current and the strong men at the oars, was already standing out to sea. It was a bitter moment for Aeetes. In a frenzy, he lifted up his hands to the gods calling on them to witness these outrageous deeds. And on the spot he threatened his whole people with dire pains if they should fail to lay their hands on his daughter. Whether they found her on land or caught the ship while still on the high seas, they must bring her to him, so that he might satisfy his lust for revenge.

Thus the king thundered; and on the self-same day the Colchians launched their ships, equipped them, and put out. One might have taken their immense armada for an endless flight of birds, flock after flock, breaking the silence of the sea.

From *The Voyage of Argo* by APOLLONIUS OF RHODES

This is one of the stories (or legends) which almost everyone knows and many people like to re-tell it in their own words.

Under the title 'The Treasure Seekers' re-tell it in your own words. You may like to do it just to please yourself, or you might have in mind a story for younger children, say 7 or 8 years old.

Opposite is a monster from a mediaeval stained glass window in St. Mary's Church, Fairford, Gloucestershire. Satan has two heads, one of which is swallowing the damned souls.

Reflect on the matter of witches and witchcraft. (Medea in this story was very different from the old hags of popular belief and fairy tale.) Then discuss with yourself in the pages of your English book whether witches are to be believed in or not; whether it is likely that people have the powers that are claimed for witches, and what your own views are and why you hold them.

Here is a poem called 'Snakecharmer.' Medea's song might have been something like this.

When you have read it aloud, using several voices to bring out its hypnotism, write a poem yourself, any poem.

Snakecharmer

As the gods began one world, and man another,
So the snakecharmer begins a snaky sphere
With moon-eye, mouth-pipe. He pipes. Pipes green.
    Pipes water.

Pipes water green until green waters waver
With reedy lengths and necks and undulatings.
And as his notes twine green, the green river

Shapes its images around his songs.
He pipes a place to stand on, but no rocks,
No floor: a wave of flickering grass-tongues

Supports his foot. He pipes a world of snakes,
Of sways and coilings, from the snake-rooted bottom
Of his mind. And now nothing but snakes

Is visible. The snake-scales have become
Leaf, become eyelid; snake-bodies ~~~~ ~~
Of ~~~ ~~~~~

~~~~ ~~ snakes!
And snakes there were, are, will be—till yawns

Consume this piper and he tires of music
And pipes the world back to the simple fabric
Of snake-warp, snake weft. Pipes the cloth of snakes

To a melting of green waters, till no snake
Shows its head, and those green waters back to
Water, to green, to nothing like a snake.
Puts up his pipe and lids his moony eye.

SYLVIA PLATH

C

p

M

v

I
v
s
v
a
c
l
a
t
(

(
`
;

'No, we didn't know, there wasn't any sign or notice we could see,' Richard said innocently.

'I think I'd better phone the police and tell them about it,' he said in a threatening way. This statement made my heart turn over for a second – we'd be in serious trouble if he did. He made us walk towards the pavilion and he said, 'Have you been here before.'

'Yes,' we replied, 'for sport, we didn't know we were trespassing,' I said desperately.

'All right then,' he said, 'but if I catch you hanging around here again when you shouldn't be, I'm warning you, I'll give you the punishment you deserve, a fine maybe.' He said this waving his finger quickly up and down at us and then let us go.

'Now get out of here,' he shouted at the top of his voice which made me jump. He then let fly an unexpected kick at Richard, which would have hit him had he not quickly jumped aside. We both then began running for the main entrance which led into Magpie Hill.

On the way home Richard said to me, 'I bet he wouldn't have phoned the police.'

'I'm not so sure myself,' I said. Then we began laughing and talking over it all.

KENNETH *aged 12½*

For discussion

Both Graham's and Kenneth's writing are reminiscences not fiction; do you think they would have been improved if the writers had introduced any of the stock characters of fiction — parents or schoolmasters, smugglers or thieves?

Which do you prefer reading, fiction or true stories?

Which do you prefer writing, fiction or reminiscences?

Suggestions for writing

1. *Away from home.*

2. *A visit to relations.*

3. *A disappointing trip.*

4. *You decide to spend a day in your holidays getting lost: what preparations would you make for such an adventure? Write a story about what might have happened and how you felt about it.*

5. *Inside the cave.*

6. *Exploring woods.*

7. *The journey from home to school: familiar people and familiar things.*

8. *Creatures I have encountered in my life.*

9. *The bus that lost itself.*

And here is a poem about a day out from the city on a bicycle. It is by a Russian poet.

On a Bicycle

Under the dawn I wake my two-wheel friend.
Shouting in bed my mother says to me,
'Mind you don't clatter it going downstairs!'
I walk him down he springing step to step:
those tyres he has, if you pat him flat-handed
he'll bounce your hand. I mount with an air
and as light a pair of legs as you'll encounter,
slow into Sunday ride out of the gates,
roll along asphalt, press down on the pedals,
speeding,   fearless,

      ring,

        ring,

          ring

get clear of Moscow, frighten a one-eyed cock
with a broken tail, lend a boy a spanner
(his hair a white mane) drink brown kvas
passing Kuntsevo in a cloud of dust,
lean up against the kvas tank (warmed with sun
hot on my back). The girl who's serving gives me
a handful of damp change from a damp hand,
won't say her name, 'You're artful all you boys . . . '
I smile 'So long . . . '
Riding to a cottage, to a friend, I gather
speed and swish away again on the road.
Flinging along my happiness my fever,
incapable of breaking out of it,
overtaking the lorries on the road
taking each of them in a single swoop
flying behind them through cut open space
hanging on them uphill. Yes I know.

It's dangerous. I enjoy it. They hoot
and lean out and ....

.... day I'll learn how to ride.
And I spring down at a deserted
ancient lodge by the roadside,
in dim forest light I break lilac,
twine it with ivy on to the handlebars.
Flying on, flying,
sticking my face down into dark blossom,
get into the city not quite worn out.
Switch on the lamp and switch off the light.
I put my bunch of lilac into water,
set the alarm to go at eight o'clock,
sit at the table
     write
       these lines.

       YEVGENY YEVTUSHENKO

*Can you write 'Some lines' about a day out, on foot, on a bicycle, in a bus,
in a car, in an aeroplane, in a space-ship even?*

diaries

Diaries are entirely one's own business. One writes them as one wants (and spells and punctuates them as one wishes!), and people try out different ways of writing to suit their feelings and the things they want to say: lists, descriptions, notes, exact records, poems for instance.

(*a*) Here are a few extracts from the holiday diary of a girl of twelve and a half called Anna. She was with her parents on a motoring-camping holiday in Europe and she felt she wanted to keep a record of this expedition. She kept a day by day record and put down all sorts of things that happened or that specially interested her.

Anna enjoyed writing but she was bad at spelling. As her diary was not meant to be published this did not matter, so she uses any word she wants to whether she can spell it or not. However, since some of it is now in print here, the spelling has been corrected. Anything *published* should be as well presented as possible.

... After St Seine l'Abbaye we climbed the hill to Cetres; on top there
was a lot of wheat and woods. We went down
side there

by me

It is our domain
And none can enter,
Cars may go,
To Dijon and afar,
But none shall stop
In our rocky land.
We have beauty
Of rocks and bareness
Of green shaded trees,
We have our stream,
Ours not yours.

... We camped in a site near Vougeot. I had everything in my tent
ready by ten past five. The camping site was near the main road. The
ground was very hard, but a man lent us a tent mallet. It was made of
rubber and very good. Some people at the site had a dog. At about half
past five we went for a walk through the fields. We passed masses of
grapes, some were going purple but most of them were green. By the
side of the path there were some very fine teazles. We kept on hearing
a scurrying of feet through the grass. We saw potatoes, and other root
crops. We walked up a hill to a willow tree and then turned left towards
a village. We came out onto a road and met a blind unfriendly dog. As
we walked through the village it began to rain, first softly, then harder.
On the way out of the village we saw a little brown goat . . . .

... When I woke up and poked my head out of my tent I saw a most adorable black kitten being led about on a piece of string by two children. I got up at a quarter past seven. We made our own breakfast at the camping site. I had cocoa, bread and butter, and marmite. We got away by twenty five to ten. Before we left I took a photograph. ...

... I must be getting lazy; I hardly did any writing. We drove up the valley towards Yugoslavia. There was a very large river-bed that was mostly dry. The road was beside the railway and river. There were signs saying Austria 'this way', and Yugoslavia 'this way'. We got some lard in a small village about five or four miles from Yugoslavia. The valley was very green. We entered Yugoslavia at a quarter past eleven, having not come very high. ...

... After some conversation with two people who only talked Serbo-Croat, Czech and Dutch Daddy found that we were allowed to camp anywhere. We got a spot right by the lake. Almost as soon as we had got the tents up it started to rain so I went inside my tent and did some writing. From my tent I could see the wooden diving board that jutted out into the lake. It stopped raining quite soon. On the other side of the lake I could see the mountains rising. They were rocky and tree-covered. At about half past seven we went to dinner. ...

Mainly discussion

Read this part of the diary carefully.

What things does she notice?

Which of these things catches your attention or interests you?

Do you find it interesting to read as a whole, or rather tedious?

At what point do you get bored with it (if you do)?

Try keeping a diary yourself for a few days to see what things you put in yours.

After some days of this kind of recording Anna got bored with it. Although they kept moving to different places she found i

Shou

ı nat
pecki
that ı
stars.

*I am no longer going to keep an account,
but am still going to write*

ACCOUNT PAGE

1. Got up at a $\frac{1}{4}$ to eight.
2. Had breakfast in camp.
3. After breakfast read D.C.[1]
4. Played knuckle-bones, whistle and solitaire.
5. Wrote.
6. Went for a walk with Mum and Dad.
7. We got our shopping for lunch.
8. We had soup, boiled egg and Yoghurt.
9. I read D.C.
10. We went out in a rowing boat. It cost about 1/- for about $\frac{3}{4}$ hr.
11. I wrote.
12. I went to the shop for cards.
13. I wrote.
14. I got my tent ready.
15. I read D.C.
16. We went for a long walk to dinner.
17. Got to bed by half past nine.

[1] David Copperfield

All that is in this diary really happened and the places are real; it is a true record, but there is matter here for a lot of stories. All stories are partly true anyway. One very wet morning when all the children were mooning round indoors and longing for the rain to stop, someone suggested that everyone should write a story and offered a prize for the best one to be chosen by vote when they had all been read out. The children (and grown-ups) went off and wrote for some time and then sat round in the sitting room to read their stories. They were a mad collection of adventurous stories, but a lot of them were about smugglers and mines and ruined engine houses, and there was an escape down a wire hawser and a chase through caves with a crossway and one villain was dashed to death by leaping down steps which had been washed away. Fact and fiction had been woven together in every story.

Suggestions for writing

1. *If these passages from a holiday diary suggest a story to you, write one.*

2. *Write about something new that you encountered while you were away from home.*

3. *Make a 'Holiday Book' by putting together eight or ten of these pieces by different members of the class. Include some stories or poems or informative pieces about the places if this seems to make a more interesting book. Photographs and illustrations too, if you like.*

4. *Make a book about a neighbourhood, with a map and notes showing your discoveries. It might be a book about your school and its neighbourhood made by a group of children, or it might be your own book of the neighbourhood you live and play in — and make discoveries in. If you haven't made many discoveries yet, can you start now? Is there a river or canal? What is its route? Is there a park or any wild places? Are there any ruins or old buildings? What do you know about them? Is there a museum? What are the smallest buildings like? What are the largest? What kind of short cuts are there in your area? Can you find signs of different customs and ways of life fossilized in the houses, such as cellars, foot-scrapers, signs in walls, mounting blocks, bread ovens, 'copper' chimneys, horse troughs, pumps, wells, etc.*

5. *Find about a square yard of garden, hedge, old brick wall, pathway or track, bush, or trunk of a large tree, and look at it very carefully. Since you are using your eyes as a close-up lens on a camera, you ought to see a lot of things that you don't normally see. Write everything down you notice — shape, colours, texture, small living things, movements, everything in fact. You may find you get tired with writing before you have written down everything you discover.*

(c)   A marine biologist describing the creatures that inhabit sandy beaches writes: *In the sands almost all is hidden. The only clues to the inhabitants of most beaches are found in winding tracks.* . . . Here is her account of the secret life of the beaches:

Bearing on its surface only the wave-carved ripple marks, the fine traceries of sand grains dropped at last by the spent waves, and the scattered shells of long-dead molluscs, the beach has a lifeless look, as though not only uninhabited but indeed uninhabitable. In the sands almost all is hidden. The only clues to the inhabitants of most beaches are found in winding tracks, in slight movements disturbing the upper layers, or in barely protruding tubes and all but concealed openings leading down to hidden burrows.

The signs of living creatures are often visible, if not the animals themselves, in deep gullies that cut the beaches, parallel to the shore line, and hold at least a few inches of water from the fall of one tide until the return of the next. A little moving hill of sand may yield a moon snail intent on predatory errand. A V-shaped track may indicate the presence of a burrowing clam, a sea mouse, a heart urchin. A flat ribbonlike track may lead to a buried sand dollar or a starfish. And wherever protected flats of sand or sandy mud lie exposed between the tides, they are apt to be riddled with hundreds of holes, marked by the sign of the ghost shrimps within. Other flats may bristle with forests of protruding tubes, pencil thin and decorated weirdly with bits of shell or seaweed, an indication that legions of the plumed worm, Diopatra, live below. Or again there may be a wide area marked by the black conical mounds of the lugworm. Or here at the edge of the tide a chain of little parchment capsules, one end free and the other disappearing under the sand, shows that one of the large predatory whelks lies below, busy with the prolonged task of laying and protecting her eggs.

But almost always the essence of the lives, the finding of food, the hiding from enemies, the capturing of prey, the producing of young, all that makes up the living and dying and perpetuating of this sand-beach fauna – is concealed from the eyes of those who merely glance at the surface of the sands and declare them barren.

For most of the fauna of the sand beaches, the key to survival is to burrow into the wet sand, and to possess means of feeding, breathing and reproducing while lying below reach of the surf. And so the story of the sand is in part the story of small lives lived deep within it, finding in its dark, damp coolness a retreat from fish that come hunting with the tide and from birds that forage at the water's edge when the tide has fallen. Once below the surface layers, the burrower has found not only stable conditions but also a refuge where few enemies threaten. Those few are likely to reach down from above – perhaps a bird thrusting a long bill into the hold of a fiddler crab – a sting ray flapping along the bottom, ploughing up the sand for buried molluscs – an octopus sliding an exploring tentacle down into a hole.

From *The Edge of the Sea* by RACHEL CARSON

*Look through your own English book or folder of work and put a pencil
mark in the margin to mark where you have used description.*

*Then make a list of the purposes of these attempts to capture something
about the world around you or the world inside your head.*

Your list might read something like this:

My feelings about a place I visited on holiday.

What a place looked like.

How a fish moves or how you bait up a fishing line.

*Details of something I want to remember, for example, the markings on
a newt or a cat.*

*What a particular piece of apparatus was like, for example for temporarily
capturing and ringing wild birds or a 'Scalextric' set.*

Details of a person's clothes and jewelry.

*What you **thought** but didn't utter.*

(*d*)   Here is a piece by a schoolboy called 'The Rocket'. Read it and discuss
the different things he describes in it. (Don't overlook the inside world of
his feelings.)

We decided to go to the fair just to look around and save our money.
Richard had ten shillings and I had a pound so I gave him five shillings
to make us even. Before we got there we could see the parachute, the
octopus and something we hadn't ever seen before called a Rocket. It had
two rockets fixed on both ends of some girders. While one rocket would
be on the ground the other would be opposite, high up in the air. This
would go round and round very fast and Richard and I thought that when
the rocket in the air would move down to the ground the people inside
would end up upside down. But we were wrong, the rocket twisted on its
way up and way down so it did a sort of twisting dive bomb when it went
down, and the opposite when it was going up.

As soon as Richard saw this he suggested us going on it. My sister
had said to me it was really frightening when she first went on it so I

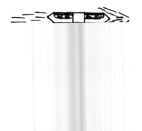

long, for not many people went on this. We got in the red rocket and were strapped down tightly with a safety belt. Then we slowly went up; we went right onto our back then went upright again. We stayed here till the other rocket was full up.

We started off slowly while the Rolling Stones record 'Satisfaction' began blaring out from the loudspeaker. As we went down I pushed hard against the rail I was holding onto so as to stop myself falling out. As we speeded up the sound of the machinery and of the air rushing past us slowly drowned the music till we couldn't hear it. By now we were going so fast that my heart began to turn over and I started to feel I wanted this to end. Then the rocket quickly slowed down till it stopped. Now I had time to admire the view, I could see so many things which looked quite small – all the side shows and I had a bird's eye view of the big wheel with the swimming pool behind it. I could watch the tiny bathers slowly moving about.

But soon it started up again in the opposite direction though it speeded up quickly this time and was going so fast that I kept coming off the seat. If it wasn't for the seat belt I would almost certainly have fallen out. That horrid thought of the seat belt breaking kept coming in my mind. Richard, who was laughing all the time, began sliding helplessly towards me and soon I was really cramped. I also laughed, keeping my fear away and I often wondered whether Richard was doing the same thing. At last my ordeal ended. We began slowing down and I could hear the music slowly getting louder. I got out of the rocket with great relief and I would never go on that again I said to myself assuringly, although Richard wanted me to go again with him, but I didn't.

E

People

For discussion and writing

Write on 'Myself' at 12, or 13, or 14, or whatever age you are.

Find a partner who is a friend and write a similar piece about him or her, and get him to write about you (i.e. an autobiographical and a biographical account).

Compare these two accounts; discuss what is in one and not in the other. How true is each?

Clearly the whole of yourself will not have been captured either in your piece of autobiography or your friend's piece of biography. What kind of thing has been left out in each?

Who knows more about you, your friend or yourself?

(a) Here is a rather short piece of autobiography by a girl called Linda, and a longer one by a boy called Peter.

Myself

I am a girl; my name is Linda. I am 13 years 10 days: I am 5 feet 2 in. I have fair long hair. I'm considered attractive and have blue eyes. When I smile I show my teeth. I like smart, fitted clothes, which are unusual.

I'm keen on sports, especially running, cricket, netball and other games. I also like to watch stock-car racing, boxing, wrestling and ice hockey.

I like gay, fast music. I don't like opera or ballet, I detest needlework. I find reading an interesting hobby; especially school books and mysteries.

On T.V. I like panel games, singers, comedian, I also like plays. I like animals and possess 5 budgerigars, 2 hens are in breeding, 1 cat. I like acting and miming. I also like swimming, I like new clothes, and new shoes. I love jewellery.

LINDA

Myself

I am a school boy and I live in the country and I enjoy it very much. At school my favourite subject is Chemistry and last term I did very well in this subject. When I was eleven years old I sat for an examination to this school and I was very pleased when I passed. I like games especially football in which I play full-back.

In the summer holidays I go to work on a farm near to where I live. There, I drive a tractor in the harvest field and I enjoy it very much. There are other boys of my age who work there with me and we have a great deal of fun when the men are cutting corn as there are a great deal of rabbits in this part of the country.

I live eight miles away from school and therefore I have to catch a bus to school or go by train. I leave home in the mornings at eight o'clock and the bus arrives at school at half past eight.

I have brown hair and am of average height. In the evenings when I have finished my homework I play cricket in a meadow near our house with some other boys.

The house in which I live is two miles from the nearest village although there are several houses nearby. I am very keen on gardening and I also keep rabbits.

I have not yet made up my mind as to what I am going to do when I leave school. I have had many ideas but after I have thought about them more seriously I have rejected them. When I was a small boy I wanted to drive a train but now I do not think I should like to.

I am fond of reading books and I always look forward to my Birthday and Christmas as my parents buy me some as they know I like reading.

I have one sister who is older than me but I have no brothers. This sometimes makes me wish I had a brother as many of the boys that I know of have some.

I have been to hospital twice with a dislocated elbow which in both cases was caused while playing football. In spite of this, however, I still

with these pieces.

Out of all the things you could say about yourself, or a friend, how do you choose what to put down?

Do you think you have succeeded in getting 'under the skin' in your account of the complicated person (you) who has been living his own history for 12, or 13 or 14 years?

(*b*) Here is a passage by a great novelist about himself and his brother when they were boys. You can see him struggling to understand himself and his brother – to get 'underneath the skin'.

My Elder Brother

I was only a year and some months younger than Volodya; we grew up, studied and played together. No distinction of elder and younger was made between us; but just about the time I am speaking of I began to realize that I was no companion for him, either in age, in interests or in ability. It even seemed to me that Volodya himself was aware of his superiority and was proud of it. This idea (it may have been a wrong one) was inspired by my vanity – which suffered every time I came in contact with him. He was better than I in everything: at games, at lessons, in arguments and in manners, and all this estranged me from him and occasioned me moral anguish which I could not understand. If I had said frankly when Volodya was given tucked linen shirts for the first time that I was vexed at not having shirts like that, I am sure I should have felt happier and not thought every time he arranged his collar that it was only done to annoy me.

What tormented me most was that it sometimes seemed to me Volodya understood what was going on inside me but tried to hide this.

But perhaps my sensitiveness and tendency to analyse deceived me in this case. It may be Volodya did not feel at all as I did. He was impulsive, candid and fickle in his enthusiasms. Carried away by the most diverse interests, he flung himself into them heart and soul.

He would suddenly conceive a passion for pictures, himself take up painting, spend all his money buying them and beg them of his drawing-master, of papa and of grandmamma. Then it would be a rage for curios with which to adorn his table, collecting them from every room in the house; or a mania for novels, which he obtained on the sly and read all day and all night . . . . I could not help being enticed by his hobbies but I was too proud to imitate him and too young and not independent enough to choose a line for myself. But there was nothing I envied so much as Volodya's happy big-hearted disposition, which showed itself most strikingly when we quarrelled. I always felt that he was behaving well but I could not do likewise.

Once when his passion for ornaments was at its height I went up to his table and there accidentally broke an empty brightly-coloured little scent-bottle.

'Who asked you to touch my things?' demanded Volodya, coming into the room and seeing how I had upset the symmetry of the different treasures on his table. 'And where is the scent-bottle? You must have. . . .'

'I knocked it over by accident and it broke. What does it matter?'

'Do me the favour – never *dare* touch my things again,' he said, putting the pieces of the broken flask together and looking at them sorrowfully.

'And you please don't issue orders,' I retorted, 'that's all. What's there to talk about in that?'

And I smiled, though I did not feel in the least like smiling.

'Yes, it's nothing to you but it does matter to me,' pursued Volodya, jerking his shoulder, a gesture he had inherited from papa. 'He goes and breaks it, and then laughs, the nasty little *brat*!'

'I'm a little brat; and you're big but you're stupid.'

'I am not going to quarrel with you,' said Volodya, giving me a slight push. 'Go away.'

'Don't push!'
'Get away!'
'Don't push, I tell...

...thought as I left the room. 'We
...for good.'

We did not speak to each other till evening. I felt myself in the
wrong and was afraid to look at him, and could not settle to do anything
all day. Volodya, on the contrary, did his lessons well, and after dinner
talked and laughed with the girls as usual.

As soon as afternoon lessons were over I left the room. I was too scared
and uncomfortable and ashamed to be alone with my brother. After
our history lesson in the evening I took my exercise books and started
towards the door. As I passed Volodya, though I wanted to go up to him
and make friends, I scowled and put on an angry expression. At that
moment Volodya raised his head and with a faintly perceptible good-
naturedly derisive smile looked me full in the face. Our eyes met and
I knew that he understood me, and knew that I knew that he understood
me; but some irresistible feeling made me turn away.

'Nicky!' he said in a most natural voice without a scrap of pathos.
'Don't be cross any more. Forgive me if I offended you.'

And he held out his hand.

Something that welled higher and higher seemed to be pressing my
chest and hindering my breathing; but this only lasted a second; tears
came to my eyes, and I felt better.

'Forgive . . . m-me, Vol-dya,' I stammered, squeezing his hand.
Volodya looked at me as if he could not make out at all why there should
be tears in my eyes.

LEO TOLSTOY

Discuss or write about *an incident in which you needed someone to understand how you behaved without an explanation, or an incident when you were puzzled by someone's behaviour.*

Clearly one can capture much more of a person when you write about what they do as well as what they look like.

Linda wrote very briefly about her appearance and the things she liked. We don't know anything about her dislikes. Peter told us a bit more — a little about where he lived and something about his thoughts about his future. Tolstoy tells us about his brother's superiority in all sorts of things, about his own jealousy and how they both *behaved* on one occasion. Probably we know more about people from what they *do* than any other way.

Now write a much fuller piece *either about yourself or about a friend (or both) in which you use all the ways you can of getting this character on to paper.*

(*c*) Here are two more passages for you to read and discuss. Both are by young people writing about an old person. John wrote his in his school-leaving examination, and Valerie wrote hers in a book she began to write when she was in the sixth form and which has now been published. Both writings are a mixture of autobiography and biography.

A Character I shall never forget

He was a short, fat man. To anybody else he would appear to be a most inconspicuous person, but to me he was one of the most favoured people of my life. You see, he was a fellow angler, and every available time he had he would take me out and teach me the rudiments of fishing. He was very kind to me, always bringing me spare tackle, although he was an Old Age Pensioner. I never did really get down to talking to him about his age, but I would say that he was over seventy.

His features were old and wizened his hands were gnarled like the roots of an old oak tree and they were hardened to all weathers. He was fairly well built, not fat, but plump if I may use the word. On his head he always wore the same old cap, indeed I have never seen him without it. He had a huge pair of thigh waders that almost covered him and invariably he had a very old overcoat around his shoulders. The tackle really brought out his true character: he had a b...

he scrubbed...

...at 6.30 in the morning we caught ...coach and set off for Bures on the Suffolk Stour. When we reached the Stour, and got down to the bank I found to my amazement, and delight, that he had brought a beautiful twelve foot match rod for me to use. I tackled up as fast as I could, and immediately started 'trotting down' in the fast flowing water. After a while I put down my rod and looked round to see how my benefactor was getting on. There he was, sitting on his stool, his face an ashen grey. I ran over to one of the club members. He came running over and set off at once to find a doctor in the nearby town. When he got back it was too late, he was dead. The doctor told us all that he had died of a heart attack.

Perhaps you will now see why I will never forget this person. I can never forget him; he has become a part of my life, and as I walk down to the riverside he will be with me walking by my side.

JOHN *aged 15*

Gran

Nevertheless, I liked Gran; she was so different from Mum. Because Mum left for work early in the morning I would go downstairs and talk to Gran while waiting to go to school. She sat in her armchair before the fire, wearing an old red dressing-gown, cooking her breakfast; she toasted bread on a fork, or held a rasher of bacon before the flames with one hand catching the drips of fat on a slice of bread which she held in her other hand. When it was cooked she put it on a plate which had already been used twice that morning: first for Steve's breakfast of bacon and mushrooms and then, when he left for work, grandad cleaned the plate with a slice of bread while waiting for his bacon and eggs to be dished up. The over-worked plate was smeared with yolk and bits of bacon curled round the edge. While Gran ate I did all the talking. I told her about school.

'We're learning French now, Gran. Quelle heure est-il? D'you know what that means?'

'Gawd knows.'

'It means: What's the time?'

'Oh does it. Can't see the point meself. Steve says they all talk English in every country, and 'e's seen almost every country on 'is bike, so what's the point? But tell me some more about that science teacher of yours.'

I envied Gran sitting in her chair with Nigger at her feet, toasting her breakfast in her warm, sleepy kitchen. I wished I could be her and not have to go to school, while she kept wishing she were my age. Her motto was 'Here today, gone tomorrow.' Mum said it was bad for me to listen to her morbid talk, but I was fascinated by tales of hospitals, funerals, and deaths.

'This woman 'ad no inside. She 'ad to live on boiled eggs and water, and 'er 'usband 'e 'ad no arms, blown off in the war they was, so 'e 'ad to manage with two 'ooks. Turned you up to look at 'im, but the funny thing is they both lived to a ripe old age, whereas 'is brother was a big 'ealthy bloke, strong as 'orse 'e was, never 'ad a day's illness in 'is life. One day 'e 'ad 'is dinner, big eater 'e was, 'e 'ad steak and kidney pud, that was his favourite grub, an' 'e says to his wife: "I think I'll take the dog for a walk in the park." So 'e goes out. But 'e never came back. Dropped down dead outside the baker's 'e did. Just like that.'

While she talked to me, she washed her face and hands in a large mixing bowl which she stood on the kitchen table and was filled to the brim with boiling water. The red, strong-smelling soap rested on a saucer while she covered her face with a creamy pink lather, then sluiced it off, cupping her hands several times with water and sounding, as she put her face into it, as though she were drinking a bowl of soup. With water dripping from her chins and her eyes stinging with soap, she groped around blindly for the towel, tugging first at the tablecloth, than at the curtains, until she realised that it was still hanging on the line over the range.

'Give us the towel, there's a good girl,' she'd say. 'Quick now. It doesn't matter if you can't find it, anything 'ill do, so long as it's not yer Grandad's combinations.'

It took her about half an hour to dress herself because she wore so many layers of clothes; petticoat upon petticoat, all of different colours and different lengths, waited in a queue to move up nearer to her skin each morning, and each was fastened by dozens of hooks and buttons.

'Yer need plenty of clothes when yer gets to my age, because yer feel the cold somethin' terrible yer do. Goes straight to yer bones it does and gives yer rheumaticks if yer don't wrap proper.'

Finally she combed her grey, greasy hair that was usually lank, but if she was going to a special jumble sale that day, or to her old age pensioners' club, she forced it to curl by using her iron curling tongs. She would sit in her arm-chair and wait for the tortuous tongs to turn red-hot in the fire then, catching a strand of hair in a scorching grasp, she twisted the tongs round and round until they could go no further. For a few seconds they were held taut while she waited for the miracle to happen.

'Does it hurt, Gran?'

'Not 'alf,' she said. 'Burnin' me brains out, it is, but it's worth it. The 'otter the tongs the longer me curls stay in.'

'Won't your hair catch alight?'

'It will if I keep 'em in too long. There, I think I'm done now,' and she pulled out the tongs leaving behind a long grey, sizzling sausage.

VALERIE

(d)   And here are two poems; one about Smith, and one called 'A Boy's
Head' but it might...

But then, there's more talent in the world
Than simply scholastic attainments!

On the Rugby field he declined to kick the squashed football,
And blushed when admitting he didn't quite know how.
The attempts at Soccer proved disastrous,
He ran with the ball, cradled in his trembling arms.
The master clasped his head, and screeched in frozen horror.
And Smith, aware of some mistake, stomped off the field,
Cursing the comrades, who forgot to inform him
                                    of the nature of the game.
But then, an entirely sports-minded population would be
                                    dull indeed.

He heard a rendering of Chopin's[1] third sonata,
And unfortunately whistled shrilly, instead of applauding,
The disgusted glances from his neighbours failed to deter him,
As he continued to express his delight in Chopin's fine music!
But then a world of musicians would certainly be boring.

But when all was considered,
Smith was just not the type for the School Head Prefect.

LINDA aged 14

[1]Pronounce literally Chop/ins.

A Boy's Head

In it there is a space-ship
and a project
for doing away with piano lessons.

And there is
Noah's ark,
which shall be first.

And there is
an entirely new bird,
an entirely new hare,
an entirely new bumble-bee.

There is a river
that flows upwards.

There is a multiplication table.

There is anti-matter.

And it just cannot be trimmed.

I believe
that only what cannot be trimmed
is a head.

There is much promise
in the circumstance
that so many people have heads.

MIROSLAV HOLUB

What do you think about these poems?

Do they also tell you something about the writers?

Try writing some poems about people.

Creatures

(*a*) Here are two descriptions of pigeons.
Discuss the differences in the two writings.

Pigeon
(Columba palumbus palumbus)

DESCRIPTION. Whole upper-parts greyish blue; breast brown-purple merging into ashy blue-grey of belly; neck with a patch of white (absent in young). L. 16–17 ins.

FIELD CHARACTERS. More heavily built and generally lighter than Stock-Dove or Rock-Dove; slower wing beat in flight, when a white patch at side of wing is conspicuous; long tail; in large flocks during winter; love call thrice-repeated 'kuk-ooe-roo, coo-oo', ending with a brief 'kuk!.'

NEST. On any tree or bush, sometimes buildings. Breeding season very variable, from March to September.

DISTRIBUTION. Resident; generally distributed; also passage migrant.

N. H. JOY

Pigeons

They paddle with staccato feet
In powder-pools of sunlight,
Small blue busybodies
Strutting like fat gentlemen
With hands clasped
Under their swallowtail coats;
And, as they stump about,
Their heads like tiny hammers
Tap at imaginary nails
In non-existent walls.
Elusive ghosts of sunshine
Slither down the green gloss
Of their necks an instant, and are gone.

From a poem by RICHARD KELL

*Make two columns and head them 'general view' and 'personal view' Write
any points you can*

(*b*) Here are two short passages written by schoolchildren about crabs.
Discuss which is the more scientific, and why.

1

Looking into the pool I saw a little creature methodically encircling the
rocky bottom. Upon seeing its waving pincers I thought to myself, 'a
crab'.

Suddenly it dodged into a small opening in the rocks and so, for a
minute, was lost to sight. Disturbed sand rose mistily from the cave
mouth, and then, like an armoured car emerging from a smoke-screen,
it re-appeared with some small victim wriggling desperately in the
grasp of one of the fearsome pincers. It was soon over and the tiny
creature was engulfed.

Its hunger appeased, it slowly moved towards the cave from whence
it had first appeared.

KENNETH

2

A crab is a marine animal which lives on the sea bed. It is usually found
in the shallow water along the coast-line. The crab is really an amphibious
creature, for it can live equally well on land or sea. They like to dig down
into the sand on the beach, and you only know they are there when you
feel a pair of pincers clinging to your toe. Their really favourite spots
are in a shallow pool, or in the mud which is left when the tide ebbs.

The crab is one of the unusual sea species. It has a hard shell encasing the whole of its body. This is for protection, because the flesh inside the case is very tender and delectable, and sea creatures are not the only crab eaters.

JUNE

For writing

In the course of the next few days take a careful look at some creature; notice all you can about it.

Write a scientific description of it.

You may want to describe its appearance, the way it moves, its habitat, its food, its home-making behaviour, etc., and you may find it useful to use lists or diagrams as well as sentences and paragraphs.

Suggestions:
Domestic pets.
Insects.
Farm animals.
Zoo animals.
Creatures from the Biology Lab.
Wild animals or birds.

Collect together a number of these in a folder so that they would make an exhibition of the fauna of your area, or if you are interested in foreign parts do one for an area you don't know; this will not be truly scientific

because all your information will be second-hand and you will not be able

as gruesomely as you can; the chants and prophesies are easy to learn.

A cleft in the hill almost in the form of a room, the abode of the three witches. A cauldron is set on a red fire.

(Thunder. Enter the three Witches)

First Witch. Thrice the brinded cat hath mew'd.
*Second Witch.*Thrice, and once the hedge-pig whined.
Third Witch. Harper cries 'Tis time, 'tis time.
First Witch. Round about the cauldron go;
           In the poison'd entrails throw.
           Toad, that under cold stone
           Days and nights has thirty-one
           Swelter'd venom sleeping got,
           Boil thou first i' the charmed pot.
All.   Double, double toil and trouble.
           Fire burn, and cauldron bubble.
*Second Witch.*Fillet of a fenny snake,
           In the cauldron boil and bake;
           Eye of newt and toe of frog,
           Wool of bat and tongue of dog,
           Adder's fork and blind-worm's sting,
           Lizard's leg and howlet's wing.
           For a charm of powerful trouble,
           Like a hell-broth boil and bubble.
All.   Double, double toil and trouble;
           Fire burn, and cauldron bubble.

Third Witch. Scale of dragon, tooth of wolf,
Witches' mummy, maw and gulf
Of the ravin'd salt-sea shark,
Root of hemlock digg'd i' the dark,
Liver of blaspheming Jew,
Gall of goat, and slips of yew
Sliver'd in the moon's eclipse,
Nose of Turk and Tartar's lips,
Add thereto a Tiger's chaudron
For the ingredients of our cauldron.

All. Double, double toil and trouble;
Fire burn, and cauldron bubble.

Second Witch. Cool it with a baboon's blood,
Then the charm is firm and good.

First Witch. By the pricking of my thumbs,
Something wicked this way comes.
Open locks,
Whoever knocks!

From *Macbeth* by WILLIAM SHAKESPEARE

Act IV, *Scene* 1

Shakespeare's witches were making a horrible brew in their cauldron, throwing in bits of various animals:

fillet of fenny snake;
eye of newt;
toe of frog;
blindworm's sting (i.e. a slow-worm: this looks like a snake but in fact has no poison and is harmless to human beings);
leg of lizard;
wing of owl;
tongue of adder.

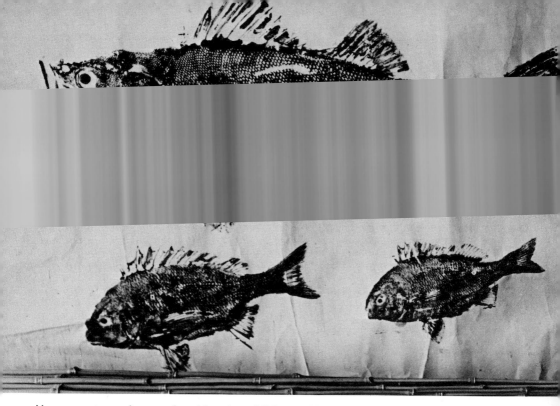

Here are two pieces of writing by children who handled some of these same sort of creatures, and liked them.

Newt

Very rainy, dull and wet. Today I made a fishing net, not to catch fish but newts. I caught six. I picked out the ones I thought best. I kept three and let the others go. There were lots of newts in the pond today. I daresay they like this kind of weather.

The three newts I caught, two were a bright orange on the belly with big black spots all over, the other one was smaller and was a muddy colour and its belly was a bright orange with very small spots on it. I mean the spots on this one were only on the belly not all over. The one I got yesterday was a dark yellow ochre.

All afternoon I sat watching them, I think they are very interesting things.
SCHOOLBOY

Slow-worm

A long scaly body slides along, the bronze scales gleaming in the sunlight, the streamlined head with small round dark eyes shining as it turns towards the sun, – a rounded nose on the end of the body. A thin layer of skin flashes over his eye as he blinks. His tongue flicks out to catch a fly, but he misses. It rises, and as it does so , its body goes rigid. It goes limp again when it lies on the floor. It gets knotted, but soon crawls out of this peculiar position, its body expanding and contracting as it breathes, from head to tail, from fat to thin.

ANTHONY

For writing

1. *Describe some creature as exactly as you can.*

2. *Write about a creature you dislike.*

3. *Discuss (in writing) the kind of dislikes people have for certain creatures; consider where these dislikes come from and whether they are deserved or not. What makes a creature hateful or frightening to people?*

4. *Write a story about a wild animal.*

5. *Write a fable (see Appendix 7)*

Discuss the different kinds of 'truth' that you find in each of these writings.

(d)   ## Preparing Racing Pigeons

It was about half past five, as I went down to the loft, the weather was fine, the wind was in the East. I loocked out accross the sky and said to my self I hope it stays as fine as this. After fidling around in my pocket I finally found my key and opened the lock. The usualy rumpus happened, My big black Cock Bird called Sulky Sam jumped on my shoulder, and started to pick my ears in his usual way, this earned him the name of Sulky Sam. I picked him up of my shoulder and loocked at him carefully, he was one of six candates, two of which would race. I loocked into his eyes, and grunted contentidly, it was good and bright, and the core was beautifully white. I ran my hand gently down his

First correct this piece for the printer. (See page 239.)
Then read it aloud.
Now discuss its quality as writing.
Has he captured the look and feel of the pigeons?
Does he convey his feelings about birds?
How do you know he is a specialist and knows a lot about racing pigeons?
What sort of words and sentences does he use?
Do you like the way he writes?
Do you consider this writing is more 'English' or 'Biology'?
Is it scientific or personal writing?

(e) Here is a story about a pigeon.
Read it together with some of the stories written about a wild animal (see
   page 96).
Consider what is in yours that is not in this one, and vice versa.

A Peace of a Pigeon

I am writing this just over an hour after it happened, while it is still fresh
in my mind.

What a lovely day this has been. The temperatures went soaring into the
upper seventies, and after spending a more or less relaxing afternoon
doing a bit of athletics, I felt that Monday, although the first working

day of the week, had been very enjoyable. Nothing had gone wrong, to speak of, – and I knew it could not last.

It did not.

I was returning home by bike from seeing the triplets of one of my grandma's goats. The only billy of the three kids had had to be killed and I had found it accidentally after looking under a paper bag. This did not have much effect on me as I already knew of its death.

As I began to sail down the hill from the farm, my eye still felt sore from poking it when getting a fly out earlier. Also the hill, I was now going down, I had always called Fly Hill due to the numerous clouds of flies, gnats, midges and other insects which seem to always be there. And so for the next two hundred yards of fairly straight but narrow road, which I had gone down on the average once a week for ten years, I had my eyes slightly open to check the way for about one tenth of the distance, and closed for the rest. Simultaneously or because of, as I opened my eyes a bird flapping madly was broad-siding into my front wheel.

I braked, skidded to a halt, and jumped off my bike. The bird, a large (at least eighteen inch wingspan) wood pigeon was scrambling for all it was worth into the undergrowth up the ten foot bank. Then it lay still, tangled in the bramble stems. I stood there looking.

An uncanny feeling went through me. A sudden anticlimax – quietness – after the sound of wind rushing past my ears, after the screeching of the brakes, after the frantic flapping of the pigeon's wings: silence and comparatively stillness, just the wind bending the young new, leaves.

My first instinct was to free the bird, although a condemned pest, from nature's own trap of bramble thorns. I scrambled up the bank and caught hold of a dead ash twig. I returned to the spot where the bird lay. I pushed the twig through the foliage just in front of its head. The pigeon at once began to scramble out, and fell down the bank. I was surprised when it did not immediately fly off with the noise of a rattle at a football match.

Perhaps it is recovering from shock was my first thought. But I was soon proved wrong: when once it began to walk it stumbled on practically every fourth step. Then it lay still.

I had a problem: to leave it to its misery and certain death from slow

starvation, or to put it out of its pain with one or several swift blows (which
I had always been brought up to beli

...y senses came back to me. It must be in more pain
than ever now. And so I hit it another three times.

Its head, with the neck broken, dropped. The eye I could see fell out.
From under its head blood, thick and bright red, oozed over the grit of
the road and stopped.

Again it was quiet. I stood shaking slightly. The light breeze blew one –
and only – one – down-feather for a couple of yards down the road.

Although I am by no means a religious person, I prayed to God that
I had done right.

Standing there I reviewed the situation: One dead pigeon near the
middle of the road; Me, the murderer, or saviour (your choice). I could
not leave it there. I scrambled up the bank to get more twigs as I had
forgotten which end of the stick had touched the pigeon. In doing so I
was stung by nettles and so I rubbed dock on to remove the irritation.

Back on the road I pushed with the aid of the twigs the bird to the bank.
I threw the twigs away, grabbed my bike, and flew off down the rest of
the hill, narrowly missing a car but I was past caring now.

The last mile home was also eventful. A car suddenly pulled up in front
of me and stalled. I narrowly missed it but in changing gear rapidly afterwards I made the chain come off the front cog. The spring in my
derailleur gears began to unwind causing havoc with the loose chain. The
result in plain language was 'my gears got bent.'

After reaching home I spent another half an hour mending them and
now I have only four out of five working. While I tried to correct the gears
I had plenty of time to work out the cause of the chain coming off in the
first place. Other than the obvious one – too loose a chain, I believe there

is another. I believe God revenges on a sin that you have committed by letting or making something unpleasant, however small, happen.

I am not complaining about the revenge, but I am puzzled by what it was revenge on. I do not know.

I just hope it was for something other than the killing of that pigeon.

IAN

(f) Here is a poem called 'Cactus'.

It is certainly not scientific writing.

Discuss whether it is more or less than the truth.

Cactus

'They're vicious,
That's what they are.'
Said the woman.
'I'm not 'aving 'em
In my house!'
Tall, green and spiky
Invading from the desert.
Long and thin,
Deadly monsters
'Take 'em to the Zoo,
Anywhere, nasty, mean-looking
Objects they are!'
Stealing a living from
The reluctant stony earth
In the tiny pot,
Weapons of a secret planet,
Marching erect.
No breeze could ever
Whisper round leaves
While they tremble.
Cold and stony silent,
The cactus takes possession
Of the suburban window-sill.

PAT

(a) Here is a story which comes from the Maoris of New Zealand. Man

showed Ma-ui where the sky and the horizon met. Flashes were to be seen there. 'They are from the teeth of the Goblin Goddess, Great-Hina-of-the-Night,' he told Ma-ui. 'She is your great ancestress. She vanquishes all creatures, for she brings all creatures to death. She will vanquish you, my child.' Then Ma-ui said, 'Let us both go to her fearlessly; let us take the heart out of her body, and so end her power of bringing death to all creatures.' But his father would not go to where Great-Hina-of-the-Night was.

Ma-ui called for companions, and the little birds of every kind assembled to go with him – the robin and the lesser robin, the thrush and the yellow-hammer and the water-wagtail. With the little birds Ma-ui went towards where the sky and the horizon met. They went in the evening, and as they went they saw the flashing of the teeth of the Goblin Goddess. Her teeth were of volcanic glass. Her mouth was wide-shaped, like the mouth of a fish. Her hair floated all around her as sea-weed floats in the sea. Her eyes shone through the distances.

He saw her and was afraid; even great Ma-ui was made afraid by the Goblin Goddess, Great-Hina-of-the-Night. But he remembered that he had told his companions that he would find a way of giving everlasting life to men and to all creatures. He thought and thought on how he could come to her and take the heart out of her body.

She was sleeping, and Ma-ui prepared to enter her terrible open mouth and take the heart out of her body and give her heart to all the creatures of the earth to eat.

Then he said to the birds, 'O my little companions, do not laugh, do not make a sound, when you see me go into the mouth of this Goblin Goddess. Laugh, make sounds if you will when you see me come out

101

bearing the heart of my ancestress, Great-Hina-of-the-Night.' The little birds that gathered around him, shivering, said, 'Oh, our brave master, we will not laugh, we will not make a sound. But, oh, take care of yourself, Master.'

Ma-ui twisted the string of his weapon around his waist. He stripped his clothes off. The skin of his legs and hips was mottled like that of a mackerel from the tattoo-marks that had been cut upon it by the chisel of Uetonga. He stood there naked, and then he went within the jaws of Great-Hina-of-the-Night. He passed the fearful teeth that were sharp like volcanic glass. He went down into her stomach. He seized upon her heart. He drew it out, and he came back as far as her jaws. He saw the sky beyond her jaws.

A little bird that often laughed tried hard not to laugh when it saw him go within the jaws of the Goblin Goddess. It twisted up its mouth to prevent its laughing. And then it laughed – little Ti-waka-waka, the water-wagtail – laughed its merry note. The Goblin Goddess opened her eyes. She started up. She caught Ma-ui between her fearful teeth, and she tore him across. There was darkness then, and the crying of all the birds. Thus died Ma-ui with the Meat of Immortality in his hands. And since his death no one has ventured near the lair of Hina-nui-te-po, the Goblin Goddess.

From *Myths of the World* by PADRAIC COLUM

For discussion

...ne behind these names?

In what ways is man an animal?

In what ways is man different from 'creatures'?

In the past people of all ages enjoyed listening to stories of magic and mystery. Nowadays such stories are chiefly read by children. Do you like fairy tales, myths, and ghost stories? Do you think science-fiction and detective stories are twentieth century fairy stories?

For writing

Imagine you were one of the companions who went with Ma-ui to find the Goblin Goddess in the evening where the sky and the horizon met. Write as full an account as you can of how you came upon her, what she looked like, and how you came back to the land after the death of Ma-ui.

Rewrite the story of any myths you know (and like) as tales for younger children.

Make up some new stories of this sort to explain anything in the world that you don't understand.

You might make a collection of these to go in a folder under the title 'Twentieth-century Myths'.

The carved stone cat opposite is guarding a Buddhist temple in Japan.

(*h*) Here is part of a twentieth-century story about a man who wakes up one morning to find he has become an insect.

Metamorphosis

As Gregor Samsa awoke one morning from uneasy dreams he found himself transformed in his bed into a gigantic insect. He was lying on his hard, as it were armour-plated, back and when he lifted his head a little he could see his dome-like brown belly divided into stiff arched segments on top of which the bed-quilt could hardly keep in position and was about to slide off completely. His numerous legs, which were pitifully thin compared to the rest of his bulk, waved helplessly before his eyes.

What has happened to me? he thought. It was no dream. His room, a regular human bedroom, only rather too small, lay quiet between the four familiar walls. Above the table on which a collection of cloth samples was unpacked and spread out – Samsa was a commercial traveller – hung the picture which he had recently cut out of an illustrated magazine and put into a pretty gilt frame. It showed a lady, with a fur cap on and a fur stole, sitting upright and holding out to the spectator a huge fur muff into which the whole of her forearm had vanished.

Gregor's eyes turned next to the window, and the overcast sky – one could hear raindrops beating on the window gutter – made him quite melancholy. What about sleeping a little longer and forgetting all this nonsense, he thought, but it could not be done, for he was accustomed to sleep on his right side and in his present condition he could not turn himself over. However violently he forced himself towards his right side he always rolled on to his back again. He tried it at least a hundred times, shutting his eyes to keep from seeing his struggling legs, and only desisted when he began to feel in his side a faint dull ache he had never experienced before.

O God, he thought, what an exhausting job I've picked on! Travelling about day in, day out. It's much more irritating work than doing the actual business in the warehouse, and on top of that there's the trouble of constant travelling, of worrying about train connexions, the bed and irregular meals, casual acquaintances that are always new and never

the alarm-clock ticking on the chest. It was half past six o'clock and the hands were quietly moving on, it was even past the half hour, it was getting on for a quarter to seven. Had the alarm-clock not gone off? From the bed one could see that it had been properly set; of course it must have gone off. Yes, but was it possible to sleep quietly through that ear-splitting noise? Well, he had not slept quietly, yet apparently all the more soundly for that. But what was he to do now? The next train went at seven o'clock; to catch that he would need to hurry like mad and his samples weren't even packed up, and he himself wasn't feeling particularly fresh and active. Gregor really felt quite well, apart from a drowsiness that was utterly superfluous after such a long sleep, and he was even unusually hungry.

As all this was running through his mind at top speed without his being able to decide to leave his bed – the alarm-clock had just struck a quarter to seven – there came a cautious tap at the door behind the head of his bed.

'Gregor,' said a voice – it was his mother's – 'it's a quarter to seven. Hadn't you a train to catch?'

That gentle voice! Gregor had a shock as he heard his own voice answering hers, unmistakably his own voice, it was true, but with a persistent horrible twittering squeak behind it like an undertone, that left the words in their clear shape only for the first moment and then rose up reverberating round them to destroy their sense, so that one could not be sure one had heard them rightly. Gregor wanted to answer at length and explain everything, but in the circumstances he confined himself to saying: 'Yes, yes, thank you, mother, I'm getting up now.' The wooden door between them must have kept the change in his voice from being noticeable outside, for his mother contented herself with this statement and shuffled away. Yet this brief exchange of words had made the other members of the family aware that Gregor was still in the house, as they had not expected, and at one of the side-doors his father was already knocking, gently, yet with his fist.

'Gregor, Gregor,' he called, 'what's the matter with you?' And after a little while he called again in a deeper voice: 'Gregor! Gregor!'

At the other side-door his sister was saying in a low, plaintive tone: 'Gregor? Aren't you well? Are you needing anything?'

He answered them both at once: 'I'm just ready,' and did his best to make his voice sound as normal as possible by enunciating the words very clearly and leaving long pauses between them. So his father went back to his breakfast, but his sister whispered: 'Gregor, open the door, do.' However, he was not thinking of opening the door, and felt thankful for the prudent habit he had acquired in travelling of locking all doors during the night, even at home.

His immediate intention was to get up quietly without being disturbed, to put on his clothes and above all eat his breakfast, and only then to consider what else was to be done, since in bed, he was well aware, his meditations would come to no sensible conclusion. He remembered that often enough in bed he had felt small aches and pains, probably caused by awkward postures, which had proved purely imaginary once he got up, and he looked forward eagerly to seeing this morning's delusions gradually fall away. That the change in his voice was nothing but the precursor of a severe chill, a standing ailment of commercial travellers, he had not the least possible doubt.

To get rid of the quilt was quite easy; he had only to inflate himself a little and it fell off by itself. But the next move was difficult, especially because he was so uncommonly broad. He would have needed arms and hands to hoist himself up; instead he had only the numerous little legs which never stopped waving in all directions and which he could not control in the least. When he tried to bend one of them it was the first to stretch itself straight; and did he succeed at last in making it do what he wanted, all the other legs meanwhile waved the more wildly in a high degree of unpleasant agitation. 'But what's the use of lying idle in bed,' said Gregor to himself.

He thought that he might get out of bed with the lower part of his body

moved his head towards the edge of the bed. That proved easy enough, and despite its breadth and mass the bulk of his body at last slowly followed the movement of his head. Still, when he finally got his head free over the edge of the bed he felt too scared to go on advancing, for after all if he let himself fall in this way it would take a miracle to keep his head from being injured. And at all costs he must not lose consciousness now, precisely now; he would rather stay in bed.

But when after a repetition of the same efforts he lay in his former position again, sighing, and watched his little legs struggling against each other more wildly than ever, if that were possible, and saw no way of bringing any order into this arbitrary confusion, he told himself again that it was impossible to stay in bed and that the most sensible course was to risk everything for the smallest hope of getting away from it. At the same time he did not forget meanwhile to remind himself that cool reflection, the coolest possible, was much better than desperate resolves. In such moments he focused his eyes as sharply as possible on the window, but, unfortunately, the prospect of the morning fog, which muffled even the other side of the narrow street, brought him little encouragement and comfort. 'Seven o'clock already,' he said to himself when the alarm-clock chimed again, 'seven o'clock already and still such a thick fog.' And for a little while he lay quiet, breathing lightly, as if perhaps expecting such complete repose to restore all things to their real and normal condition.

But then he said to himself: 'Before it strikes a quarter past seven I must be quite out of this bed, without fail. Anyhow, by that time someone will have come from the warehouse to ask for me, since it opens before seven.' And he set himself to rocking his whole body at once in a regular rhythm, with the idea of swinging it out of bed. If he tipped himself out in that way he could keep his head from injury by lifting it at an acute angle when he fell. His back seemed to be hard and was not likely to suffer from a fall on the carpet. His biggest worry was the loud crash he would not be able to help making, which would probably cause anxiety, if not terror, behind all the doors. Still, he must take the risk.

When he was already half out of the bed – the new method was more a game than an effort, for he needed only to hitch himself across by rocking to and fro – it struck him how simple it would be if he could get help. Two strong people – he thought of his father and the servant girl – would be amply sufficient; they would only have to thrust their arms under his convex back, lever him out of the bed, bend down with their burden and then be patient enough to let him turn himself right over on to the floor, where it was to be hoped his legs would then find their function. Well, ignoring the fact that the doors were all locked, ought he really to call for help? In spite of his misery he could not suppress a smile at the very idea of it.

He had got so far that he could barely keep his equilibrium when he rocked himself strongly, and he would have to nerve himself very soon for the final decision since in five minutes' time it would be a quarter past seven – when the front-door bell rang. 'That's someone from the warehouse,' he said to himself and grew almost rigid, while his little legs only jigged about all the faster. For a moment everything stayed quiet. 'They're not going to open the door,' said Gregor to himself, catching at some kind of irrational hope. But then of course the servant girl went as usual to the door with her heavy tread and opened it. Gregor needed only to hear the first 'good morning' of the visitor to know immediately who it was – the chief clerk himself. What a fate, to be condemned to work for a firm where the smallest omission at once gave rise to the gravest suspicion! Wouldn't it really have been sufficient to send an apprentice to inquire – did the chief clerk himself have to come? And more through the agitation caused by these reflections than through any act of will Gregor swung himself out of bed with all his strength. There was a loud thump, but it was not really a crash. His fall was broken to some extent by the carpet, his back, too, was less stiff than he thought, and so

to hear it.

'Gregor,' said his father now from the left-hand room, 'the chief clerk has come and wants to know why you didn't catch the early train. We don't know what to say to him. Besides, he wants to talk to you in person. So open the door, please. He will be good enough to excuse the untidiness of your room.'

'Good morning, Mr Samsa,' the chief clerk was calling amiably meanwhile.

'He's not well,' said his mother to the visitor, while his father was still speaking through the door. 'He's not well, sir, believe me. What else would make him miss a train! The boy thinks about nothing but his work. It makes me almost cross, the way he never goes out in the evenings, he's been here the last eight days and has stayed at home every single evening. He just sits there quietly at the table reading a newspaper or looking through railway time-tables. I must say I'm glad you've come, sir; we should never have got him to unlock the door by ourselves; he's so obstinate; and I'm sure he's unwell, though he wouldn't have it to be so this morning.'

'I'm just coming,' said Gregor slowly and carefully, not moving an inch for fear of losing one word of the conversation.

'I can't think of any other explanation, madam,' said the chief clerk. 'I hope it's nothing serious.'

'Well, can the chief clerk come in now?' asked Gregor's father impatiently, again knocking on the door.

'No,' said Gregor.

In the left-hand room a painful silence followed this refusal, in the right-hand room his sister began to sob.

Why didn't his sister join the others? She was probably newly out of bed and hadn't even begun to put on her clothes yet. Well, why was she crying? Because he wouldn't get up and let the chief clerk in, because he was in danger of losing his job, and because the chief would begin dunning his parents again for the old debts? Surely these were things one didn't need to worry about for the present. Gregor was still at home and not in the least thinking of deserting the family. At the moment, true, he was lying on the carpet and no one who knew the condition he was in could seriously expect him to admit the chief clerk. But for such a small discourtesy, which could plausibly be explained away somehow later on, Gregor could hardly be dismissed on the spot. And it seemed to Gregor that it would be much more sensible to leave him in peace for the present than to trouble him with tears and entreaties. Still, of course, their uncertainty bewildered them all and excused their behaviour.

'Mr Samsa,' the chief clerk called now in a louder voice, 'what's the matter with you? Here you are, barricading yourself in your room, giving only "yes" and "no" for answers, causing your parents a lot of unnecessary trouble and neglecting – I mention this only in passing – neglecting your business duties in an incredible fashion. I am speaking here in the name of your parents and of your chief, and I beg you quite seriously to give me an immediate and precise explanation. You amaze me, you amaze me. I thought you were a quiet, dependable person, and now all at once you seem bent on making a disgraceful exhibition of yourself. For some time past your work has been most unsatisfactory; this is not the season of the year for a business boom, of course, we admit that, but a season of the year for doing no business at all, that does not exist, Mr Samsa, must not exist.'

'But, sir,' cried Gregor, beside himself and in his agitation forgetting everything else, 'I'm just going to open the door this very minute. A slight illness, an attack of giddiness, has kept me from getting up. I'm still lying in bed. But I feel all right again. I'm getting out of bed now. Just give me a moment or two longer! I'm not quite so well as I thought, but I'm all right, really. How a thing like that can suddenly strike one down! Only last night I was quite well, my parents can tell you, or rather I did

some sign of it. Why didn't

himself upright by means of it. He meant actually to open the door, actually to show himself and speak to the chief clerk; he was eager to find out what the others, after all their insistence, would say at the sight of him. If they were horrified then the responsibility was no longer his and he could stay quiet. But if they took it calmly, then he had no reason either to be upset, and could really get to the station for the eight o'clock train if he hurried. At first he slipped down a few times from the polished surface of the chest, but at length with a last heave he stood upright; he paid no more attention to the pains in the lower part of his body, however they smarted. Then he let himself fall against the back of a near-by chair, and clung with his little legs to the edges of it. That brought him into control of himself again and he stopped speaking, for now he could listen to what the chief clerk was saying.

'Did you understand a word of it?' the chief clerk was asking; 'surely he can't be trying to make fools of us?'

'Oh dear,' cried his mother, in tears, 'perhaps he's terribly ill and we're tormenting him. Grete! Grete!' she called out then.

'Yes, mother?' called his sister from the other side. They were calling to each other across Gregor's room.

'You must go this minute for the doctor. Gregor is ill. Go for the doctor, quick. Did you hear how he was speaking?'

'That was no human voice,' said the chief clerk in a voice noticeably low beside the shrillness of the mother's.

'Anna! Anna!' his father was calling through the hall to the kitchen, clapping his hands, 'get a locksmith at once!' And the two girls were already running through the hall with a swish of skirts – how could his sister have got dressed so quickly? – and were tearing the front door open.

There was no sound of its closing again; they had evidently left it open, as one does in houses where some great misfortune has happened.

But Gregor, was now much calmer. The words he uttered were no longer understandable, apparently, although they seemed clear enough to him, even clearer than before, perhaps because his ear had grown accustomed to the sound of them. Yet at any rate people now believed that something was wrong with him, and were ready to help him. The positive certainty with which these first measures had been taken comforted him. He felt himself drawn once more into the human circle and hoped for great and remarkable results from both the doctor and the locksmith, without really distinguishing precisely between them. To make his voice as clear as possible for the decisive conversation that was now imminent he coughed a little, as quietly as he could, of course, since this noise too might not sound like a human cough for all he was able to judge. In the next room meanwhile there was complete silence. Perhaps his parents were sitting at the table with the chief clerk, whispering, perhaps they were all leaning against the door and listening.

Slowly Gregor pushed the chair towards the door, then let go of it, caught hold of the door for support – the soles at the end of his little legs were somewhat sticky – and rested against it for a moment after his efforts. Then he set himself to turning the key in the lock with his mouth. It seemed, unhappily, that he hadn't really any teeth – what could he grip the key with? – but on the other hand his jaws were certainly very strong; with their help he did manage to set the key in motion, heedless of the fact that he was undoubtedly damaging them somewhere, since a brown fluid issued from his mouth, flowed over the key and dripped on the floor.

'Just listen to that,' said the chief clerk next door; 'he's turning the key.'

That was a great encouragement to Gregor; but they should all have shouted encouragement to him, his father and mother too: 'Go on, Gregor,' they should have called out, 'keep going, hold on to that key!' And in the belief that they were all following his efforts intently, he clenched his jaws recklessly on the key with all the force at his command. As the turning of the key progressed he circled round the lock, holding on now only with his mouth, pushing on the key, as required, or pulling it down with all the weight of his body. The louder click of the finally yielding lock literally quickened Gregor. With a deep breath of relief

when he heard the chief clerk utter a loud "Oh!" —

gust of wind – and now he could see the man, standing as he was nearest to the door, clapping one hand before his open mouth and slowly backing away as if driven by some invisible steady pressure. His mother – in spite of the chief clerk's being there her hair was still undone and sticking up in all directions – first clasped her hands and looked at his father, then took two steps towards Gregor and fell on the floor among her outspread skirts, her face quite hidden on her breast. His father knotted his fist with a fierce expression on his face as if he meant to knock Gregor back into his room, then looked uncertainly round the living-room, covered his eyes with his hands and wept till his great chest heaved.

Gregor did not go now into the living-room, but leaned against the inside of the firmly shut wing of the door, so that only half his body was visible and his head above it bending sideways to look at the others. The door leading to the hall was open, and one could see that the front door stood open too, showing the landing beyond and the beginning of the stairs going down.

'Well,' said Gregor, knowing perfectly that he was the only one who had retained any composure, 'I'll put my clothes on at once, pack up my samples and start off. Will you only let me go? You see, sir, I'm not obstinate, and I'm willing to work; travelling is a hard life, but I couldn't live without it. Where are you going sir? To the office? Yes? Will you give a true account of all this? Stand up for me in the firm. Travellers are not popular there, I know. Sir, don't go away without a word to me to show that you think me in the right, at least to some extent!'

But at Gregor's very first words the chief clerk had already backed away and only stared at him with parted lips over one twitching shoulder. And while Gregor was speaking he did not stand still one moment but stole away towards the door, without taking his eyes off Gregor, yet only an inch at a time, as if obeying some secret injunction to leave the room. He was already at the hall, and the suddenness with which he took his last step out of the living-room would have made one believe he had burned the sole of his foot. Once in the hall he stretched his right arm before him towards the staircase, as if some supernatural power were waiting there to deliver him.

Gregor perceived that the chief clerk must on no account be allowed to go away in this frame of mind if his position in the firm were not to be endangered to the utmost. His parents did not understand this so well; they had convinced themselves in the course of years that Gregor was settled for life in this firm, and besides they were so preoccupied with their immediate troubles that all foresight had forsaken them. Yet Gregor had this foresight. The chief clerk must be detained, soothed, persuaded and finally won over; the whole future of Gregor and his family depended on it! If only his sister had been there! She was intelligent; she had begun to cry while Gregor was still lying quietly on his back. And no doubt the chief clerk, so partial to ladies, would have been guided by her; she would have shut the door of the flat and in the hall talked him out of his horror. But she was not there, and Gregor would have to handle the situation himself. And without remembering that he was still unaware what powers of movement he possessed, without even remembering that his words in all possibility indeed in all likelihood, would again be unintelligible, he let go the wing of the door; pushed himself through the opening; started to walk towards the chief clerk, who was already ridiculously clinging with both hands to the railing on the landing: but immediately, as he was feeling for a support, he fell down with a little cry upon all his numerous legs. Hardly was he down when he experienced for the first time this morning a sense of physical comfort; his legs had firm ground under them; they were completely obedient, as he noted with joy; they even strove to carry him forward in whatever direction he chose; and he was inclined to believe that a final relief from all his sufferings was at hand. But in the same moment as he found himself on the floor, rocking with su̶p̶p̶r̶e̶s̶s̶e̶d̶ not far fr̶o̶m̶ h̶i̶s̶

... c̶a̶r̶p̶e̶t̶.

M̶other, Mother,' said Gregor in a low voice and looked up at her. The chief clerk, for the moment, had quite slipped from his mind; instead, he could not resist snapping his jaws together at the sight of the creaming coffee. That made his mother scream again, she fled from the table and fell into the arms of his father, who hastened to catch her. But Gregor had now no time to spare for his parents; the chief clerk was already on the stairs; with his chin on the banisters he was taking one last backward look. Gregor made a spring, to be as sure as possible of overtaking him; the chief clerk must have divined his intention, for he leapt down several steps and vanished; he was still yelling 'Ugh!' and it echoed through the whole staircase. Unfortunately, the flight of the chief clerk seemed completely to upset Gregor's father, who had remained relatively calm until now, for instead of running after the man himself, or at least not hindering Gregor in his pursuit, he seized in his right hand the walking-stick which the chief clerk had left behind on a chair, together with a hat and greatcoat, snatched in his left hand a large newspaper from the table and began stamping his feet and flourishing the stick and the newspaper to drive Gregor back into his room. No entreaty of Gregor's availed, indeed no entreaty was even understood, however humbly he bent his head his father only stamped on the floor the more loudly. Behind his father his mother had torn open a window, despite the cold weather, and was leaning far out of it with her face in her hands. A strong draught set in from the street to the staircase, the window curtains blew in, the news-papers on the table fluttered, stray pages whisked over the floor. Pitilessly Gregor's father drove him back, hissing and crying 'Shoo!' like a savage.

4.   Monsters: True Records?

evaluating evidence — logs, reports, journals — observation and argument —
no evidence needed! stories and poems

(a) On 31 August 1938 the steam tug *Arrow* was on her maiden voyage from Leith to Manchester by way of the Caledonian Canal and Loch Ness. When about $2\frac{1}{2}$ miles west of Urquhart Castle the Master, Captain William Brodie of Leith, noticed a large dark object showing above the water, 'reminding him somewhat of a whale'. Captain Brodie said afterwards:

I was astonished at the sight of so big a creature in an inland loch, for though I had heard of the Monster I had been very sceptical. I realised that this was nothing like a whale for a second dark hump appeared behind the first, and then the whole creature dived below only to reappear in a few minutes racing through the water at a terrific speed and showing about seven humps or coils. The wash was like that made by a powerful speed-boat. All the crew excepting the fireman saw the Monster.

The Master made the following entry in the ship's log:

August 30th 1938. Saw wake of a large animal to southwest while close inshore $2\frac{1}{2}$ miles from Castle Urquhart. In sight again for half a minute 4.50 p.m. Seen by all crew on deck.

Why do you think, in the log, he says 'saw wake of a large animal' and not 'saw large animal'? In his verbal account he gives quite definite details of the animal's appearance. Do you think he didn't believe his eyes? Was he afraid of being laughed at? Do you think he saw 'the wake' and jumped to the conclusion it was the Monster and would not therefore enter it in the true and exact record which a ship's log should be?

No one except the Master knows the answer to these questions but they are worth thinking about.

The 'bull' shown opposite is part of Japanese students' rag day celebration.

(*b*)   Here is another eye-witness account by the Warden of the Youth Hostel at Alltsaigh halfway down the northern side of Loch Ness. This Warden was a retired policeman of thirty years service in Invernessshire so he must have been used to giving exact reports of things seen.

One day in 1949 he was working at the back of the Hostel. 'On looking up,' said the Warden, 'I noticed a strange looking object about 800 yards away. The water was absolutely calm and the object was pretty well in a line between myself and Foyers (on the opposite side of the loch). After a minute or two the object changed in shape and what I took to be the head and neck were raised above the water and a large hump could be seen behind. The hump fitted the term popular wth other witnesses, resembling an upturned boat. I was just thinking of calling my wife and the assistant warden when the Monster sank leaving quite a surge on the surface of the loch. After a moment or two, to my surprise it came up again, I then called my assistant, Colin Cameron, who arrived in time to see three humps, each about 10 feet long, while about 10 feet separated each hump. The creature travelled along in this form its speed being at least 30 miles an hour and, believe me, it must be an enormous creature having regard to the size of the humps which stood two or three feet above the water. I then fetched binoculars from the house and had another excellent view. The skin, I thought, resembled that of an elephant. The Monster dived again, this time in the direction of Fort Augustus and did not reappear. It was a great pity that a party of cyclists from Newcastle upon Tyne had just left, for they would then have been able to see for themselves.'

On another occasion the Warden saw the Monster moving up the loch in the moonlight, and on a third he saw, as he said: 'Something like a telegraph pole advancing towards me, five feet out of the water and swaying very slightly from side to side as it came forward.'

Compare this account with the following:

Creature seen in Loch Ness on Sunday October 1st between 10 and 10.30 a.m. Duration of period of observation 12 minutes. Seen at a distance of 700–800 yards as measured on a 6-inch ordnance map. No glasses available. Day was dead calm and exceedingly clear there

can judge its head was carried about j
was not much thicker than the neck. Colour was dark, either grey or
brown.

I did not see any part of the body, but the ripples proceeding from
the neck may have obscured my view of that. As it was moving slowly
there was no great wash but just such a ripple behind it as is left by a
small rowing boat.   B. A. RUSSELL

*Try reading these two eye-witness accounts aloud. Do you believe them?
Do you find either more convincing than the other?*
Try listing the actual information given in each of these – information about
the time and place, the condition of the light and of the weather, the
splash or ripples, and the actual creature. In a separate column put any
other 'information' conveyed by remarks such as 'to my surprise', 'it was
a pity that . . .', etc. Then see how much each writer has said about
the creature itself.
Which of them makes more careful and accurate statements?

(c)   And here is what a professional zoologist wrote:

... strange to say it is just the great number of witnesses and the discrepancy of their testimony that have convinced professional zoologists that the Loch Ness Monster is not a thing of flesh and blood. . . . The only kind of being whose existence is testified to by scores of witnesses and which never reaches the dissecting table, belongs to the world of spirits. . . . I have come to the conclusion that the existence or non-existence of the Loch Ness Monster is not a problem for zoologists but for psychologists.

Can you put in your own words his reasons for not believing the existence of the monster in spite of all the eye-witnesses? Why do you think he suggests it is a problem for psychologists rather than zoologists?

The writer of the book from which these passages were taken has collected scores of such first hand accounts and interviewed as many of the eye-witnesses as she could find. What do you think about it all?

Do people tend to see what they expect to see? Do they notice things they don't expect to see? Do people's accounts of the same incident (such as a car accident) differ from one another? If so, why is this?

How are facts established (i.e. found to be true or untrue) (1) in a court of law (2) in a subject like Biology or Botany (3) in History?

(d)   The writer of the book also collected some of the expressions used to describe the creature's head and neck: like a serpent's head; like a turtle's head; like a bird in the water; like a huge swan; like a horse's head on a long neck; like a rather thick periscope; a dark column; a partly submerged telegraph pole; head dished like a terrier's; from the front flat and wide, from the side hardly wider than the neck; size of head like that of a large dog but definitely snake-like; head like an adder, same bore as neck. Further types of head mentioned in the comparison have been goat, camel, giraffe, cow, deer, horse, seal, eel, turtle, and sheep.

This is an interesting collection, and you may note that since most people have not seen the Monster, and since nothing like it exists, the eye-witnesses have to describe it in terms of what people know; they have to say it is *like* something else. This is always the way we use language about something new.

For writing

1. *An adventure story involving a monster of some sort.*
2. *An exact description of a large slug, or a garden snail, or a worm. Give details of colour, shape, texture, and movement, but make no reference*

(*a*) Here is a description of a creature written by a girl of 12. What creature, in fact, was it?

So small, yet it moves quickly with jerking movements, flicking out a forked tongue. Ready for hibernation, its mouth gapes in a sort of yawn, a most peculiar movement. . . . It scratches its head with a back leg. Its eyes close, its eyes, small dots on either side of a flat head, dots, black, alert and clear. They wander, examining the background. It moves as if searching for something, its nose down like a hound on the scent.

Its neck could be described as scraggy, like an old man's; its legs small yet perfect in every detail; tiny feet like hands with five long thin fingers with tiny claws at the end. Its body tends to get fatter in the middle and to drag on the ground as it moves. It gets thinner, it tapers down to the tail, long, (twice as long as the body) thin and pointed. Its backlegs are powerful, bent nearly always, with the same feet and claws as the front. It has a dry skin, dully coloured with brown and a dusty colour on top to match a dull ground. The underside is a bright yellow but still speckled with black. It is covered in minute scales and its tail seems to be ringed to the tip. LINDSAY

Try drawing this creature from the description. Why is this very difficult?
In fact ten of these and other creatures had been borrowed from the Biology
Lab. and the boys and girls observed and handled them and talked about

them for most of a lesson. They had previously studied them in a science lesson and they wrote exactly what they saw.

Would you call this creature a 'monster'?

Attempt a definition of a 'monster'.

Look up the word 'monster' in a dictionary and compare what it says with your definition.

Are the ideas of large size and ugliness an essential part of your definition?

What do you understand by ugliness?

Does Lindsay say, or suggest, that her creature is ugly?

(*b*) Darwin finds the fossil bones of prehistoric monsters.

Megatherium:

Huge fossil herb-eating sloth.

Mega or megalo = great } Greek
therios = wild beast

Megalonyx:

Huge fossil sloth.

onyx = claw: Greek

Scelidotherium:

Giant fossil lizard.

scelido = lizard: Latin
therios = wild beast: Greek

Pachyderm:

Thick-skinned quadruped that does not chew cud e.g. elephant.

pakhus = thick } Greek
derma = skin

Toxodon:

Extinct quadruped with strongly curved molar teeth.

toxon = bow } Greek
odon = tooth

Mylodon Darwinii:

Gigantic sloth with cylindrical teeth.

mylo = mill } Greek
odon = tooth

Darwinii = of the sub species discovered by Darwin.

one occasion, when in a boat, we were so entangled by these shallows
that we could hardly find our way. Nothing was visible but the flat beds
of mud; the day was not very clear, and there was much refraction, or
as the sailors expressed it, 'things loomed high.' The only object within
our view which was not level was the horizon; rushes looked like bushes
unsupported in the air, and water like mud-banks, and mud-banks like
water.

We passed the night in Punta Alta, and I employed myself in searching
for fossil bones; this point being a perfect catacomb for monsters of
extinct races. The evening was perfectly calm and clear; the extreme
monotony of the view gave it an interest even in the midst of mud-banks
and gulls, sand-hillocks and solitary vultures.

. . . At Punta Alta we have a section of one of these later-formed
little plains, which is highly interesting from the number and extraordinary character of the remains of gigantic land animals embedded in
it. I will here give only a brief outline of their nature.

First, parts of three heads and other bones of the Megatherium, the
huge dimensions of which are expressed by its name. Secondly, the
Megalonyx, a great allied animal. Thirdly, the Scelidotherium, also an
allied animal, of which I obtained a nearly perfect skeleton. It must
have been as large as a rhinoceros: in the structure of its head it comes,
according to Mr Owen, nearest to the Cape Anteater, but in some other
respects it approaches to the armadillos. Fourthly, the Mylodon Darwinii,
a closely related genus of little inferior size. Fifthly, another gigantic
edental quadruped. Sixthly, a large animal, with an osseous coat in
compartments, very like that of an armadillo. Seventhly, an extinct kind
of horse, to which I shall have again to refer. Eighthly, a tooth of a

Pachydermatous animal, a huge beast with a long neck like a camel, which I shall also refer to again. Lastly, the Toxodon, perhaps one of the strangest animals ever discovered: in size it equalled an elephant or megatherium, but the structure of its teeth, as Mr Owen states, proves indisputably that it was intimately related to the Gnawers, the order which, at the present day, includes most of the smallest quadrupeds: in many details it is allied to the Pachydermata: judging from the position of its eyes, ears, and nostrils, it was probably aquatic, like the Dugong and Manatee, to which it is also allied.

The remains of these nine great quadrupeds, and many detached bones were found embedded on the beach, within the space of about 200 yards square. It is a remarkable circumstance that so many different species should be found together; and it proves how numerous in kind the ancient inhabitants of this country must have been.

The remains at Punta Alta were embedded in stratified gravel and reddish mud, just such as the sea might now wash up on a shallow bank. They were associated with twenty-three species of shells, of which thirteen are recent and four others very closely related to recent forms; whether the remaining ones are extinct or simply unknown, must be doubtful, as few collections of shells have been made on this coast. As, however, the recent species were embedded in nearly the same proportional numbers with those now living in the bay, I think there can be little doubt, that this accumulation belongs to a very late tertiary period. From the bones of the Scelidotherium, including even the knee-cap, being intombed in their proper relative positions, and from the osseous armour of the great armadillo-like animal being so well preserved, together with the bones of one of its legs, we may feel assured that these remains were fresh and united by their ligaments, when deposited in the gravel together with the shells. Hence we have good evidence that the above enumerated gigantic quadrupeds, more different from those of the present day than the oldest of the tertiary quadrupeds of Europe, lived whilst the sea was peopled with most of its present inhabitants.

From *The Voyage of the Beagle* (1831–36) by CHARLES DARWIN

Discussion

Darwin's b----- --

...... about his finds

.... round them. What kind of facts does he choose
to note down?

What information beyond the actual names does a scientist gain by being
told the technical (Greek) names for the creatures? (See Appendix 4,
page 223–4.)

In the last paragraph he marshalls the evidence from the shells in the soil
where the fossils were found and from the shells in the soil of the beaches
along the coast to argue 'that the giant quadrupeds lived while the sea
was peopled with most of its present inhabitants'.

Can you sort out what his argument is and what evidence he uses to make it?

What use does he make of comparison?

Was he using judgement in coming to his conclusion?

Is he writing science or history, or both?

Suggestions for writing

A fictional story about how you made a scientific discovery.

Decide whether you will write it as:
1. A diary.
2. A narrative reported after it had all happened.
3. A story being told as it happened (i.e. in the present time).

Read some of the stories written by other people in your class and discuss
which of these forms (1, 2, or 3) you prefer for this story. Which, for
instance, allows most freedom to the writer; which seems most vivid?
Remember it is a discovery of scientific importance you make, so there
should be some specific facts and observations in it, even if it is fiction.

I

Fossil ammonites. These were soft bodied marine animals which lived in hard shells; they became extinct about 50 million years ago.

Here is an incident from Conan Doyle's *The Lost World* published in 1912.
Discuss how it compares with the story you have just written.

On the morning after our being trapped upon the plateau we began a new stage in our experiences. The first incident in it was not such as to give me a very favourable opinion of the place to which we had wandered. As I roused myself from a short nap after day had dawned, my eyes fell upon a most singular appearance upon my own leg. My trouser had slipped up, exposing a few inches of my skin above my sock. On this there rested a large, purplish grape. Astonished at the sight, I leaned forward to pick it off, when, to my horror, it burst between my finger and thumb, squirting blood in every direction. My cry of disgust had brought the two Professors to my side.

'Most interesting,' said Summerlee, bending over my shin. 'An enormous blood-tick, as yet I believe, unclassified.'

'The first-fruits of our labours,' said Challenger in his booming, pedantic fashion. 'We shall have to name it. The very small inconvenience of being bitten, my young friend, cannot, I am sure, weigh with you as against the glorious privilege of having your name inscribed in the deathless roll of zoology. Unhappily you have crushed this fine specimen at the moment of satiation.'

'Filthy vermin!' I cried.

Professor Challenger raised his great eyebrows in ...
a soothing paw upon my shoul...
'Y... ...

... ...t of that,' said Summerlee, grimly, 'for one has
just disappeared behind your shirt-collar.'

Challenger sprang into the air bellowing like a bull, and tore fran-
tically at his coat and shirt to get them off. Summerlee and I laughed so
that we could hardly help him. At last we exposed that monstrous torso
(fifty-four inches, by the tailor's tape). His body was all matted with black
hair, out of which jungle we picked the wandering tick before it had
bitten him. But the bushes round were full of the horrible pests, and it
was clear that we must shift our camp.

Hardly had we started when we came across signs that there were
indeed wonders awaiting us. After a few hundred yards of thick forest,
containing many trees which were quite unknown to me, but which
Summerlee, who was the botanist of the party, recognized as forms of
conifera and of cycadaceous plants which have long passed away in the
world below, we entered a region where the stream widened out and
formed a considerable bog. High reeds of a peculiar type grew thickly
before us, which were pronounced to be equisetacea, or mare's-tails,
with tree-ferns scattered amongst them, all of them swaying in a brisk
wind. Suddenly Lord John who was walking first, halted with uplifted
hand.

'Look at this!' said he. 'By George, this must be the trail of the
father of all birds!'

An enormous three-toed track was imprinted in the soft mud before
us. The creature, whatever it was, had crossed the swamp and had passed
on into the forest. We all stopped to examine that monstrous spoor.
If it were indeed a bird – and what animal could leave such a mark? – its

foot was so much larger than an ostrich's that its height upon the same scale must be enormous.

'But what do you make of this?' cried Professor Summerlee, triumphantly, pointing to what looked like the huge print of a five-fingered human hand appearing among the three-toed marks.

'Wealden!' cried Challenger, in an ecstasy. 'I've seen them in the clay of the Sussex Weald. It is a creature walking erect upon three-toed feet, and occasionally putting one of its five-fingered fore-paws upon the ground. Not a bird, my dear Roxton – not a bird.'

'A beast?'

'No; a reptile – a dinosaur. Nothing else could have left such a track. They puzzled a worthy Sussex doctor some ninety years ago; but who in the world could have hoped – hoped – to have seen a sight like that?'

His words died away into a whisper, and we all stood in motionless amazement. Following the tracks, we had left the morass and passed through a screen of brushwood and trees. Beyond was an open glade, and in this were five of the most extraordinary creatures that I have ever seen. Crouching down among the bushes we observed them at our leisure.

There were, as I say, five of them, two being adults and three young ones. In size they were enormous. Even the babies were as big as elephants, while the two large ones were far beyond all creatures I have ever seen. They had slate-coloured skin, which was scaled like a lizard's and shimmered where the sun shone upon it. All five were sitting up, balancing themselves upon their broad, powerful tails and their huge three-toed hind-feet, while with their small five-fingered front-feet they pulled down the branches upon which they browsed. I do not know that I can bring their appearance home to you better than by saying that they looked like monstrous kangaroos, twenty feet in length, and with skins like black crocodiles.

I do not know how long we stayed motionless gazing at this marvellous spectacle. A strong wind blew towards us and we were well concealed, so there was no chance of discovery. From time to time the little ones played round their parents in unwieldy gambols, the great beasts bounding into the air and falling with dull thuds upon the earth. The strength of the parents seemed to be limitless for

difficulty in

for it slowly lurched off through
followed by its mate and its three enormous infants. We saw
the shimmering slatey gleam of their skins between the tree-trunks, and
their heads undulating high above the brushwood. Then they vanished
from our sight.

'What will they say in England of this?' cried Summerlee at last.

'My dear Summerlee, I will tell you with great confidence exactly
what they will say in England,' said Challenger. 'They will say that you
are an infernal liar and a scientific charlatan, exactly as you and others
said of me.'

'In the face of photographs?'

'Faked, Summerlee! Clumsily faked!'

'In the face of specimens?'

'Ah, there we may have them! And put it down in your diary, my young
friend, and send it to your paper.'

'And be ready to get the toe-end of the editorial boot in return,'
said Lord John. 'Things look a bit different from the latitude of London,
young fellah-my-lad. There's many a man who never tells his adventures,
for he can't hope to be believed. Who's to blame them? For this will
seem a bit of a dream to ourselves in a month or two. *What* did you say
they were?'

'Iguanodons,' said Summerlee. 'You'll find their footmarks all over
the Hastings sands, in Kent, and in Sussex. The South of England was
alive with them when there was plenty of good lush green-stuff to keep
them going. Conditions have changed, and the beasts died. Here it seems
that the conditions have not changed, and the beasts have lived.'

'If ever we get out of this alive, I must have a head with me,' said

Lord John. 'I don't know what you chaps think, but it strikes me that we are on mighty thin ice all this time.'

I had the same feeling of mystery and danger around us. In the gloom of the trees there seemed a constant menace, and as we looked up into their shadowy foliage vague terrors crept into one's heart. It is true that these monstrous creatures which we had seen were lumbering, inoffensive brutes which were unlikely to hurt anyone, but in this world of wonders what other survivals might there not be – what fierce, active horrors ready to pounce upon us from their lair among the rocks or brushwood? I knew little of prehistoric life, but I had a clear remembrance of one book which I had read in which it spoke of creatures who would live upon our lions and tigers as a cat lives upon mice. What if these also were to be found in the woods of this lost plateau?'

(c) Here is a set of notes based on ...

... comes from the fact ... have their own territory which they guard fiercely and will fight any other Robin which enters it to the death.

An ornithologist, who studied the behaviour of robins, wrote:

The most important use of song to the robin in its territory is to advertise possession to rivals and to warn them off. But not only does the song of the robin serve as a warning prelude to a fight, but robins actually sing while fighting, interpolating vigorous song-phrases between their attacks on intruders, while the finest singing of the year is heard when one cock is trying to establish itself in the territory of another. At least in the robin, the chorus of song early on a Spring morning – often called the birds' Hymn to the Dawn – is a hymn of battle rather than of love.

From *The Life of the Robin* by DAVID LACK

Write some notes based on careful observation of:
Babies before they can walk.
Cats (not just one cat).
Sparrows.
Pigeons.
Seagulls.
Goldfish.
Budgerigars.
Hamsters.
Use any technical words that you know and which belong to the subject you choose to write notes on.

Fossil skeleton of dinosaur discovered in Mongolia, Russia, in the 1930s.

no evidence needed!

One of the most famous monsters (whom you may have read about before) was called **Grendel**. His story is found in a ninth-century Anglo-Saxon poem about the adventures of a warrior called Beowulf. Grendel lived on human flesh and raided the King's palace for his victims. Here is an account of one of his raids.

Over the misty moor
From the dark and dripping caves of his grim lair,
Grendel with fierce ravenous stride came stepping.
A shadow under the pale moon he moved,
Towards Heorot. He beheld it from afar, the gleaming roof
Towering high to heaven. His tremendous hands
Struck the studded door, wrenched it from the hinges
Till the wood splintered and the bolts burst apart.
Angrily he prowled over the polished floor,
A terrible light in his eyes – a torch flaming!
As he scanned the warriors, deep-drugged in sleep,
Loud loud he laughed, and pouncing on the nearest
Tore him limb from limb and swallowed him whole,
Sucking the blood in streams, crunching the bones.
Half-gorged, his gross appetite still unslaked,
Greedily he reached his hand for the next – little reckoning
For Beowulf. The youth clutched it and firmly grappled.

Such torture as this the fiend had never known.
In mortal fear, he was minded to flee to his lair,
But Beowulf prisoned him fast. Spilling the benches,
They tugged and heaved, from wall to wall they hurtled.
And the roof rang to their shouting, the huge hall
Rocked, the strong foundations groaned and trembled.
Then Grendel wailed from his wound, his shriek of pain
Roused the Danes in their hiding and shivered to the stars.
The warriors in the hall spun reeling from their couches,
In dull stupor they fumbled for their swords, forgetting

No man-made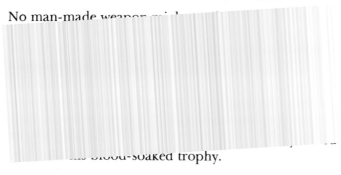

...blood-soaked trophy.

From near and far
The Danes came flocking to Heorot to behold
The grisly trophy – Grendel's giant arm
Nailed to the wall, the fingertips outspread,
With nails of sharpened steel and murderous spikes
Clawing the roof.

From *Beowulf the Warrior* by IAN SERRAILLIER

For writing

Rewrite this story—or part of it—in your own words and fill in some of the details from your imagination.

The poem goes on to tell how Beowulf set out to kill Grendel who lived at the bottom of a deep lake in lonely moorland country. The battle takes place deep under water. Write the story of this battle in prose or verse— whichever you prefer.

Or write a poem about either incident.

Write about a creature you are frightened of.

Some people hate spiders, or snakes, or bats, and sometimes even dogs or cats, or cows! Choose one you have strong feelings against.

Some people are not frightened by living things but have fears of lonely woods, or streets, or fog or being in the dark.

Write on one of these.

Do you prefer to read fact or fiction? Write about your preference and try to explain it.

Here is a story told in 1900 by a miller, who got the story from an older miller, so it must go back to the wars with Napoleon about 1800.

Bone Meal in the Flour

You all know that the old churchyard at Southery is so high that it makes the church look as if it was built in a hole. Well, that's because so many folk have been buried one on top of the other, that the church doorstep is six feet lower than the topmost body, and it's been like that for years and years. Now, Dusty who was a miller like me, told me that when he was a boy there used to be a mill standing close by the churchyard wall, and it stood there in the days when only those who'd got a few gold coins put by were allowed to be buried in the churchyard. Poor folk, and there were a lot of them, were thrown into a pit near the mill, and when one pit was full another was dug, so, in time, the poor's piece was raised as high as the mound where the mill stood. The mill, at the time I'm telling you about, belonged to the Bishop of Ely, and the miller had to pay a rent of twelve sacks of flour a year to the Bishop, who ate so much bread that he was as round as he was high; and so was the Southery parson who got three sacks of free flour a year.

At that time there was a war on with France, and my grandfather who worked the mill then was standing by the mill door when a stranger rode up on horseback. Grandfather recognised him as a chap who'd been riding all over the Fens buying up hay which he sold to the Government in London for twice the price he gave for it. He asked Grandfather why the mill wasn't working.

'There's nothing to grind,' said Grandfather, 'farmers won't sell their corn.'

'They would if you hit a high enough price,' said the chap. 'But what's under that big mound over there?'

'Bones,' said my Grandfather, 'it's the Poor's Piece; the poor have to be buried there as there's no room for them in the churchyard.'

'Who does the mill belong to?' asked the man; 'I want to buy it, bones and all.'

When he heard that it belonged to the Bishop he hurried off to Ely to see him, but the Bishop wouldn't sell.

Now out in fen [obscured] ...miller used to say, were full of corn but, though wheat was selling at three pounds a sack, the farmers were holding on, hoping to get ten shillings more. That chap paid the price they asked and soon his mill was working away day and night, if there was wind enough. Once a week he had a sack of lime delivered and he used this to bleach the bones white, and after these had gone through the crusher a bushel of them was put in the mill hopper with every bushel of corn. He sold all his flour to the government to feed the soldiers and sailors and he got twice as much for the flour as the corn had cost, so the bones and lime were all profit.

The farmers round about here were so pleased at getting such a good price for their corn that they asked the parson to hold a special service in the church; farmers came from miles away and made so much noise singing that it was a week before the jackdaws could get back into the belfry.

When the war was over the bone miller was a very rich man, but he didn't last long because the lime settled on his chest. He was taken a long way away to be buried as he'd said, before he died, that he didn't want to be put in on top of other folk in Southery churchyard; but Grandfather and the other Southery people used to say it was because he didn't want to have his bones laid too close to a flour mill in case there was another war. DUSTY MILLER

From *More Tales from the Fens* by W.H. BARRETT

For discussion

Do you think this is likely to be a true story?

> Fee, Fi, Fo, Fum
> I smell the blood of an Englishman.
> Be he alive or be he dead
> I'll grind his bones to make my bread. . .
>
> . . . sang the Giant in *Jack the Giantkiller.*

Do you think there could be a foundation of truth to this rhyme from a fairy story?

Look up the note in Appendix 4 on 'Sources of History' and read the following notice from the 'Leicester Journal' of 1802.

Note. An 'assize' was originally a *trial* of the quality and weight of things like bread, or tin ingots, or silver ingots; anything which was publicly sold and which profiteers were likely to sell at short weight or cheat over in some way. Manufacturers had to bring their goods to the assize and have them officially stamped that they were up to standard.

County of Leicester

Assize of BREAD, set for the 14th day of October 1802

	lbs	ozs	drs
The Penny Loaf Wheaten to weigh:		7	10
The Penny Loaf Household to weigh:		10	2
The Sixpenny Loaf Wheaten to weigh:	2	13	12
The Sixpenny Loaf Household to weigh:	3	12	12
The Eighteenpenny Loaf Wheaten to weigh:	8	9	4
The Eighteenpenny Loaf Household to weigh:	11	6	4

From the 20th November

Every Wheaten Loaf is to be marked with a large Roman W and every Household Loaf with a large Roman H on pain of forfeiting not more than 20/- and not less than 5/- for every loaf. To be continued until another Assize is set.

Can you interpret what lies behind this order?
Try to answer the following questions.

the real flour?

For individual study

Bone Meal in the Flour *was a spoken story not a written one. It was taken down quite recently very much as it was told, and it had been told from one generation to another for about a hundred years. Make a list of anything in this story* which shows it was a spoken story.

Does this story strike you as a true story?

To test your hunch as to whether it is likely to be true or not look up Appendix 4, page 224, 'Sources of history'. You will find you have three sources here:

1. Legend *incorporated in a fairy tale.*
2. *A story handed down orally before it was put into writing.*
3. *An* official record *of the Assize of Bread indicating that bread made of wheat was dearer than 'other kinds' of bread and making it illegal not to distinguish between these.*

Using these sources argue the case (in writing) as to whether we should believe Dusty Miller's story or not.

For discussion and reflection

Darwin spent a great part of his life on his scientific work which was a major contribution to knowledge and he was famous in his lifetime, yet, late in his life, he wrote this:

My mind seems to have become a machine for grinding general laws out of large collections of facts, but why this should have caused the atrophy of that part of the brain alone, on which the higher tastes depend, I cannot conceive. A man with a mind more highly organised or better constituted than mine, would not, I suppose, have thus suffered; and if I had to live my life again, I would have made a rule to read some poetry and listen to some music at least once every week; for perhaps the parts of my brain now atrophied would thus have kept active through use. The loss of these tastes is a loss of happiness, and may possibly be injurious to the intellect, and more probably to the general character, by enfeebling the emotional part of our nature.

Discuss as fully as you can what he meant. You need to discuss it almost word for word.
Is there anything in your own experience which makes you think you understand what he is saying?

Double-headed serpent from Mexico, 14th or 15th century.

Go and open the door.
  Maybe a dog's rummaging.
  Maybe you'll see a face,
Or an eye,
or the picture
         of a picture.

Go and open the door.
  If there's a fog
  it will clear.

Go and open the door.
  Even if there's only
  the darkness ticking,
  even if there's only
  the hollow wind,
  even if
      nothing
         is there,
go and open the door.
At least
there'll be
a draught.

MIROSLAV HOLUB

... Exploring one's Past

autobiography – turning the spotlight – comment – capturing the past

K

146

If the reminiscences of one person covered all his life from h..
to the age he was when he wrote .....
autobio....

..... who were part of your life then, and
... you reel about them?

How would you arrange your memories in writing a full-length story of
your life so far?

Here are three pieces of autobiographical writing.

1

I remember getting up late this morning
I remember carrying a slice of toast into the garage while I loaded
   my bag onto my bike.
I remember when the cat got stuck in freshly laid tar
And had to have her fur cut off.

I remember my father's funeral on Tuesday.
I remember the flowers and wreaths,
I remember the big Rolls.
I remember the men in the sitting room a few of which I did not
   know.

MARGARET *aged* 13

2

Nan and Aunt Rose shared the house, Nan and Grandad living downstairs, Aunt Rose, Uncle Jack and my cousins, Peter and Paul, upstairs,
but I always thought of it as Nan's house, since she governed everyone

in it, firmly upholding the principles of cleanliness and honesty. It was no use trying to lie to her because her blue eyes permeated your very heart and there she always managed to find the truth. After you had stammered out some story about why you were late for dinner, her eyes turned from blue to purple and she'd say: 'Your tongue must be that red hot, young lady, after telling such a tale, that I shouldn't be surprised to see it shrivel to cinders and drop out.' My tongue began to burn and I would have to blurt out the truth.

Grandad also believed in cleanliness, but before that or anything else he put his garden. He spent most of his time out there, no matter what the weather, bending over his rake, stopping every so often to tap his pipe on the sole of this shoe and refill it with tobacco taken from the pouch in the pocket of his red woollen waistcoat. When he came in to dinner he cast his beady eyes round the table, before speaking in his staccato fashion: 'Sit up, Valerie. You'll have round shoulders. Peter, show me your hands. I thought so, you filthy boy, wash them at once. Mother, there's no salt on the table. Can't you eat with your mouth closed, Valerie?'

'But it's hot, Grandad,' I explained.

'And haven't you been told that it's rude to speak with your mouth full?'

'Oh shut up, Guy Fawkes,' said Nan, sitting down. 'Leave them alone, can't you? Get on with your dinner. Always on at them, you are; getting too old, that's your trouble.'

'All right, Mother,' he replied rather meekly. 'It's for their own good, I want them to have proper table manners.'

'You're a fine one to talk about manners, you are, with that dewdrop hanging from the end of that nose of yours ever since breakfast. It's enough to put anybody off their food. Wipe it off, you dirty old man.'

Grandad always had a dewdrop hanging from his nose. Sometimes it dropped into his tea, and sometimes it dropped onto his precious lawn. That lawn was as smooth as his own bald head and just as clean. We weren't allowed to step on it without first asking him, and if we did, while he was inside the house, there would be a sudden rap at the window and he would scream: 'Get off, you young hooligans, get off, do you hear?'

'C
But
~LL

He didn't have much time for us children during the d~~
ed us at night when we ~~~~."

smal
one
movi
treas
was (

It
morr
thou;
dowr
on b(
who
the h
dowr

At
if it
insid(
sunli;
were
slowl
cover
tools
came
open(
was b
In it

... ~~u slate,
In that little red school house
I was always late.
I went there when I was a scholar
In the days of yore.
I would stand and holler
"Two and two make four".'

We made him sing the song over and over again, and stopped him every time he got the words wrong. Convinced that we were clean from our heads to our heels, he sat down in the armchair and lit his pipe. He puffed and coughed for a few minutes, wiped his eyes with a khaki handkerchief the size of a table-cloth, then, with Paul on his lap, Peter and I on the floor at his feet, he began telling one of his stories. . . .

'Now, when I was a boy I never wore such things as pyjamas, not like what you wear. Why, they were unheard of in my days,' he puffed at his pipe, his brown, broken teeth sucked and sucked, and his speech loosened up. 'No, I slept on a marble-hard bed stark naked from head to toe. Didn't have a stitch of clothing on me, not a stitch. Just you imagine lying there in the middle of winter wearing nothing but your birthday suit. I shivered myself to sleep and woke up covered with goose pimples. And it was four o'clock in the morning when I had to get up. Think of that now, four o'clock and still dark as night outside. And what did I get up for, when other folks were lying comfortable in their beds? Why, to get food, that's why.

'With my belly rumbling and nagging at me because I'd had nothing to eat since the day before, I went out hunting with my father. And think

These words made me see the cave as not merely ancient, but different from any other, a survival from another world. The rocks which touched my bare ankle seemed so different from common rock that they had a special chill and sliminess, horrible and strange; the dark green water, at which I gazed down past my father's shoulder, appeared strange even to the sight, a primitive water. I imagined that no fish could live in it. Above all, the light and noises in this cave seemed unique. The light was a pallid green, broken by flashes of dark silver or platinum from the waves outside the cave mouth, so that when my father set me down on the ledge, I saw the thin hook of his nose and the long line of his thin jaw, green on one side and lead on the other, as if the cave had changed him into a demon. Meanwhile, all round, as if to a great distance, there was a peculiar sucking noise, like those derisive kisses made by the village boys at street corners when couples passed in the twilight.

All of us had since looked into this cave at every opportunity, but only from the Shell Port. We would wade out at low tide and stare down the crack. I have seen Anketel thus, in all his clothes, wet to the armpits, gazing into the twilight with the absorbed concentration of those who peer through a fence at a murderer's house, after he has been hanged. He could see nothing, but his imagination was at work. I had told him, of course, that the cave was a million years old, older than the fish.

From *A House of Children* by JOYCE CARY

For writing

Describe how you visited a place after a long interval, three years, or four years for example. On the second visit, did it look as you remembered it? Had anything changed? Had you changed?

or Write about the younger (or the older) members of your family as they seemed to you when you were very small.

or What it was like to be a child in some period earlier than you can remember. (This will have to be based either on stories you have heard from parents or grandparents, or else from books.)

or A story beginning: When the spring came I realized that Winter had aged me.

or Choose one of the photographs and write the thoughts of this person.

capturing the past

...ay. Anyway,
, ... there they come running hobbling from
one foot to the other, hastily shifting from one foot to the other the
plumpness of their legs, feathers, flanks and down, their necks taut, their
beaks gaping, jammed together honking and hissing your only choice is
to pounce on them and yell louder than they do to scare them, they hardly
flinch and run forward honking even louder than before. You pretend to
kick them. They swerve to the side making a kind of croaking noise, but
as soon as you turn your back to run away they give you good hard nips
on the calves of your legs. You start to run to get away from there.

After the geese there are the dogs. The first is a black and white ratter
with a pointed nose, pointed ears and tiny little eyes. He is in a hallway
the door to which is always open on to the street. He is hidden in the
shadows. He waits for you to go by then he comes out barking, you turn
around to scare him, you kick him in the nose, he yelps as if he were crying
but the minute your back is turned he quietly gives you a bite in the calves.
The second dog is a ratter too, all black, smaller and faster. He doesn't
bark. He lies under a cart or against the wall in the shade. He pretends
not to look when you go by but he bites you in the calves just the same
even if you run.

When Veronique Legrand and Catherine Legrand take the road above
the village besides the geese and the dogs there are some boys who lie
in wait for you and attack you with nettles as you go by. You have
to fight them to disarm them or else they hit Veronique Legrand and
Catherine Legrand on the legs and thighs which are left bare by their short
knickers. They outnumber Veronique Legrand and Catherine Legrand
with the result that no matter what you do you get blisters all over, you

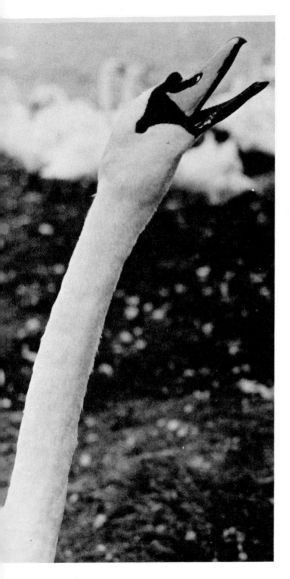

don't know how. For this reason you buy yourselves pocket knives and take the road through the middle of the village to take them by surprise. They wait concealed on the other side crouching behind a wall, you can sneak up from behind and attack them with your knives. Veronique Legrand and Catherine Legrand have the knives open in the palms of their hands, Veronique Legrand holds hers open in her left hand because she is left-handed. Catherine Legrand holds hers open in her right hand because she is right-handed. In this way they can easily advance side by side very close together, hip to hip with the knives on the outside. It will be hard to take them by surprise. The boys turn around with their nettles the instant the girls arrive. When they see Catherine Legrand and Veronique Legrand with knives they yell something you don't understand and pounce on them throwing all the brambles in their faces, on their legs, on their thighs, at once and running away. Mother confiscates the knives because the boys tattle to their parents.

From *The Opoponax* by MONIQUE WITTIG

For discussion and writing

, is all about what happens to the two girls on their way home from school and how they feel about it, and 'you', of course, means Catherine and Veronique. It is written as if the young girls were talking and thinking on paper.

Much of the work you do in school is concerned with helping you to move towards adult standards of writing and thinking. This time write something that captures you as you are now; how you see things and how you feel about them. It would be best to find your own subject, but if you want suggestions, here are some:

Going home from school.

The Shopkeeper.

Event in the playground.

A detestable visit.

Today is Saturday.

A quarrel or a fight.

It was a mad thing to do. . . .

Machines you enjoy watching.

A hole in the ground.

A person who frightens you.

The best places in your neighbourhood.

A mystery (Don't explain it, just describe it).

Things you would like to buy that are beyond your pocket money.

L

TRUTH TO TELL

Mrs Humphreys writes to the Editor of the *Padstow Echo*.
To be able to write a letter like this must surely be what learning English is all about; and it is *ordinary* English, and look what it captures!

Dear Mr Fuller,

How I do enjoy reading the Echo, so many names I recall, people and places; those who did not know or live in Padstow in my young days know nothing of it as it was. The lovely carols at Christmas sung in the quiet night, when we could lean out of the window and pick out the different voices, the penetrating and delicious smell of all the saffron cakes (made extra good for Christmas) coming from the Bakehouse, where they had been taken very early in the morning, a special oven of course, before the roasts and pasties had to go in for dinner. The thrill to me of being allowed to get up in the dark and watch mother getting the cake in the tins and sometimes being allowed to go up to the Bakehouse with them, all warm and fresh and clean inside with the warmth of the bricked-in oven heated with faggots.

Eastertide and the beautiful warm sun, the flowers everywhere, the patch of violets just inside the top Churchyard gate. The procession on Good Friday by the Choir and Clergy from the Church down to the Quay where a short Service was held and where all men bowed their heads and listened. The hymns that were always sung and old Mr Ding always wore his skull cap. All gone now I am told, oh! what a pity.

Whitsun week with the regatta, the march to Church of The Forresters, the Wesleyan Sunday School Treat on Wednesday and the Church on Thursday, the beautifully decorated waggons decorated with masses of flowers by Miss Loui Cowell and a host of helpers; the patience they must have had now that I think back. All we girls in white, shepherds' crooks with a piece of ribbon and a flower at the top, carried by the older ones, as well as the banners of the different activities of the Church and the lovely banner which headed the procession.

Lifeboat Day and the fun with Alec Hornabrook dressed like an old lady, complete with lace, mittens and parasol, being tipped out of a boat in the harbour and climbing back again. Harvest time and the scent of honeysuckle and all the other wild flowers, coming down 'School-board Hill' after father had finished for the day, on top of the last cartload, no children of this day and age can know anything of those delights

I have ....

.... g .... , ... s eye all the
things I have been writing about has made me all shaky, I feel 'pitchaired'
as me mother would have said!

Thank you again for keeping Padstow alive, and keep on the good
work.

Yours sincerely,
Ida May Humphreys

(I hope to print photos of the decorated waggons mentioned, Church,
Wesleyan, United Methodists and the shepherd girls – Editor.)

*It is said that old people have their memories and young people have their
dreams.*

*If you feel inclined to share your dreams about your future, write about
them.*

*or Write a story made up of three incidents in the life of a boy, or girl; one
when he is very small, one when he is the age you are now, and one when
he is considerably older. Make it quite clear that it is the same person.
Note: does he change as he gets older?*

*or Write about a festival of some sort – or an occasion when many people
participated. What did you do, see, hear, say, sing, etc.?*

Here are two poems about growing up – or getting a bit older – or changing in some way. Read them – more than once – perhaps discuss them, and if they start you off, write a poem.

Nursery Rhyme of Innocence and Experience

I had a silver penny
    And an apricot tree
And I said to the sailor
    On the white quay

'Sailor O sailor
    Will you bring me
If I give you my penny
    And my apricot tree

A fez from Algeria
    An Arab drum to beat
A little gilt sword
    And a parakeet?'

And he smiled and he kissed me
    As strong as death
And I saw his red tongue
    And I smelt his sweet breath

'You may keep your penny
    And your apricot tree
And I'll bring you presents
    Back from sea.'

O the ship dipped down
    On the rim of the sky
And I waited while three
    Long summers went by

Then one still morning

All round her wake
   The seabirds cried
And flew in and out
   Of the hole in her side.

Slowly she came
   In the path of the sun
And I heard the sound
   Of a distant gun.

And a stranger came running
   Up to me
From the deck of the ship
   And he said, said he

'O are you the boy
   Who would wait on the quay
With the silver penny
   And the apricot tree?

I've a plum-coloured fez
   And a drum for thee
And a sword and a parakeet
   From over the sea.'

TRUTH TO TELL

O where is the sailor
  With bold red hair?
And what is that volley
  On the bright air?

O where are the other
  Girls and boys?
And why have you brought me
  Children's toys?

CHARLES CAUSLEY

his chimney and smoke,
his view from the window.

He made himself a garden,
    his fence,
    his thyme,
    his earthworm,
    his evening dew.

He cut out his bit of sky above.

And he wrapped the garden in the sky
and the house in the garden
and packed the lot in a handkerchief

and went off
lone as an arctic fox
through the cold
unending
rain
into the world.

MIROSLAV HOLUB

Section Eight: Exploring the Past

biography — family tree — chronological order — what really happened? —
eye-witness

Part of the wall built by the Roman Emperor Hadrian in A.D. 122 as a defence against the invading Picts. It ran across the North of England from the Solway to the Tyne.

family trees

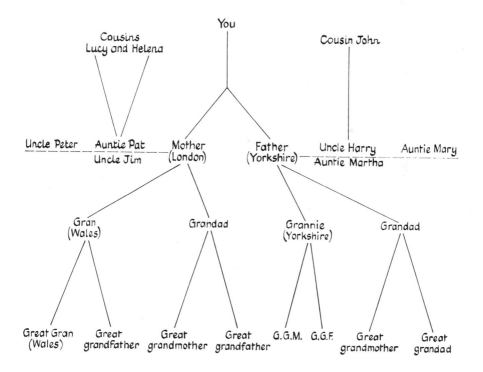

A biography is the story of someone else's life. It is made up of many shorter stories.

Tell some biographical stories about members of your family.

171

chronological order

Everyone expects to hear what happened in a story *in the order in which it happened*, i.e. in chronological order. Otherwise people can't make sense of it.

The following are all chronological records:

A diary – a personal daily record – see Anna's diary pages 51–55.

A ship's log – a ship's daily record – see the log of the *Arrow*, page 121.

A journal – either a personal daily record – see Darwin's journal, page 127, or a weekly or monthly newspaper – see the *Leicester Journal*, page 140.

Chronicles – a record continuing over a number of years – see below.

Here are some passages from the oldest written records of English history that exist. They are called *The Anglo-Saxon Chronicles*. They were written on parchment by monks in the English of their time which is so different from the English of today that they have to be translated (see Appendix 6).

Two entries from the seventh century.

A.D.

671   This year happened that great destruction among the fowls.

674   This year Escwin succeeded to the kingdom of Wessex. He was the son of Cenfus, Cenfus of Cenferth, Cenferth of Cuthgils, Cuthgils of Ceowulf, Ceowulf of Cynric, Cynric of Cerdic.

Two entries from just over a hundred years later.

A.D.

787   This year King Bertric took Edburga the daughter of Offa to wife. And in his days first came three ships of the Northmen from the land of robbers. The sheriff rode to meet them, and tried to drive them to the King's town; for he knew not what they were; and there was he slain. These were the first ships of the Danish men that sought the land of the English nation.

793   This year came dreadful fore-warnings over the land of the *Northumbrians*, terrifying the people most woefully; these were immense sheets of light rushing through the air, and whirlwinds, and fiery

A Viking ship, 80 feet long, found at Gokstad in Norway. It was built about A.D. 900.

dragons flying across the firmament. The tremendous tokens were soon followed by a great famine, and not long after, on the sixth day before the ides of January in the same year, the harrowing inroads of heathen men made lamentable havoc in the church of God in Holy island, by rapine and slaughter.

Three more entries from about a hundred years later.

878   This year about mid-winter, after twelfth-night, the Danish army stole out to Chippenham, and rode over the land of the *West Saxons*; where they settled, and drove many of the people oversea; and of the rest, the greatest part they rode down, and subdued to their will; ALL BUT ALFRED THE KING. He, with a little band, uneasily sought the woods and fastnesses of the moors. . . .

879   This year went the (Danish) army from *Chippenham* to *Cirencester*, and sat there a year. The same year assembled a band of pirates,

and sat at *Fulham by the Thames*. The same year also the sun was eclipsed one hour of the day.

882 This year went the army up along the Maese far into *Frankland*, and there sat a year; and the same year went King Alfred *out to sea with a fleet*, and fought with four ship-rovers of the Danes, and took two of their ships, wherein all the men were slain, and the other two surrendered; but the men were severely cut and wounded ere they surrendered.

A hundred years later we read:

978 This year all the oldest counsellors of England fell at Calne from an upper floor; but the holy Archbishop Dunstan stood alone upon a beam. Some were dreadfully bruised, and some did not escape with life. This year was King Edward slain, at eventide at Corfegate, on the fifteenth day before the calends of April. And he was buried at Wareham without any royal honour. No worse deed than this was ever done by the English nation since they first sought the land of Britain.

991 This year was *Ipswich* plundered; and very soon afterwards was Alderman Byrtnoth slain at Maldon. In this same year it was resolved that tribute should be given, for the first time, to the Danes, for the great terror they occasioned by the sea-coast. That was first 10,000 pounds. The first who advised this measure was Archbishop Sigeric.

994 This year came Anlaf and Sweyn[1] to London, on the Nativity of St. Mary with four and ninety ships. And they closely besieged the city, and would fain have set it on fire; but they sustained more harm and evil than they ever supposed that any citizens could inflict on them. The holy mother of God on that day considered the citizens and ridded them of their enemies. Thence they advanced, and wrought the greatest evil than ever any army could do, in burning and plundering and manslaughter, not only on the sea-coast in *Essex*, but in *Kent* and in *Sussex* and in *Hampshire*. Next they took horse and rode as wide as they would and committed un-

[1] Danish leaders

speakable evil. Then resolved the king and his council to .... l ..

What kind of things were the monks who wrote the Anglo-Saxon Chronicles interested in?

What could the entry for the year 671 have meant? (No one knows.)

What do you notice about the names of King Escwin's ancestors? Compare
the names in the pedigrees of thoroughbred racehorses.

Which of the items in the Anglo-Saxon Chronicles are you prepared to
believe, and why?

The first entry for the year 978 is a very curious one and doesn't tell us much;
what do you think actually happened?

Wooden stem-post of a Viking ship, probably 8th century.

what really happened?

Read the entry for the year 991 and discuss as fully as you can what might have taken place. Since there is nothing but a few bare facts to work on, you will have to imagine what really happened when 'Ipswich was plundered' and how Alderman Byrtnoth was killed at Maldon.

Here is a poem by a schoolgirl: she imagines what the Danish raids were like.

The Coming of the Norsemen

The war horns brayed,
Brayed like the sound of the
Breakers crashing upon the cold
North-beach
Brayed their message to all
Who would hear,
To all the world.
And the Norsemen answered,
Answered all who would
Question their power,
Their berserk madness.
They crossed the wild foam-flecked enraged sea.
The dragon prows ploughed
Through the grey-green sea.
A hundred prows, a hundred times three.
Seeming in number to rival the stars
In the sky.
So they journeyed along the gulls way
Until they saw the smooth untroubled
Waters of the Humber.
With a roar of triumph
Unmolested by the cowering guiltless
Men of the fields.
No man stood before them,

No man had the courage to resist.
Blackened charred ruins ~~~~ ~

~~~~ ~

...... the men of Essex by a tidal creek and a
~. ~y~unoth's men easily killed the Danes who tried to cross over the
narrow channel left at low tide. Then the Danes shouted across the water
that they would go away if the English gave them gold instead of spears.
Byrtnoth replied: 'This people will give you no gold but a spear, sharp
shafts and new fear and the long sword you cannot use.'

So the fight was on. Byrtnoth recklessly allowed the heathen Danes to
cross the water so they could get at the enemy, but things began to go
wrong for the English. Byrtnoth seems to have got separated from his
bodyguard who were sworn to stand by him till death, so some of the
English thought the battle was lost. Then a cowardly nobleman jumped
on to Byrtnoth's horse which was tethered near the battlefield and its
princely trappings misled many English into thinking it was their leader
who was galloping away so they broke the rank of the 'shield wall' and
began to scatter. This is how Byrtnoth was killed in the hand-to-hand
fighting.

A seafarer (Dane) hurled a spear which pierced the Earl's shield and
wounded him, but he shook the shaft out of his shield and drove it
through the neck of the proud Viking who had wounded him. Then a
Viking javelin pierced the ring-mail of his breast and as he laughed and
shouted thanks to God for such a glorious battle, yet another javelin went
into him. A young warrior by his side plucked out the bloody spear and
hurled it at the sender, killing him. Another Viking approached the
wounded Byrtnoth intending to seize his gold bracelets and armour and
ornamented sword. Then Byrtnoth drew the sword, broad and gleaming
edged and struck the Viking in the chest, but another Norseman stopped

M

the stroke and destroyed the Earl's arm, and the golden-hilted sword fell to the ground. Byrtnoth could no longer fight nor stand firm on his feet, yet he cried encouragement to his men before the heathen men hewed him down.

And the only actual record we have says: 'this year *Ipswich* was plundered; and very soon afterwards was Alderman Byrtnoth slain at Maldon.'

For writing

1. *Try filling in some of the gaps in the records by making up what you think might have happened, for instance:*
   Write a story which begins: 'He [King Alfred], with a little band, uneasily sought the woods and fastnesses of the moors. . . . ' 878.
   or *Write a story about what happened when ' . . . all the oldest counsellors of England fell at Calne from an upper floor; but the holy Archbishop Dunstan stood alone upon a beam. Some were dreadfully bruised, and some did not escape with life' 978.*
   or *Choose any other entry and write a story about what happened, using your imagination to fill in the details.*

2. *List the years (down the page) where there is a reference to the invasion of the heathen Danes. Opposite each year write short notes of what happened. You will now have an* abstract *or skeleton of the information from the chronicles about the Danish invasions. Notice: how many years they went on for; what part of England they began in and where they spread to; when the English first began to buy the Danes off.*
   Using these notes write an interesting and brief history of these invasions.
   Warning. Don't just copy out your notes; they are for you, not your readers, because the English you use will need to be more interesting than notes, and you may not use all the information and you may choose to refer to the Anglo-Saxon poems, *Beowulf* and 'The Battle of Maldon'. In short your story of the invasion should be like a body and not like a skeleton.

3. *Write brief notes on the last five years of your own life. Put the date of the year in the margin and select not more than three or four items to record for each year. What you choose to record is your own affair, but try to think of the things which seem most important or interesting to you.*

eye-witness

... my main subject, and tell you how, shortly after we had taken Damietta[1] all the sultan's horsemen assembled before the camp and attacked it from the landward side. The king and all his knights armed themselves. I, for my part, after putting on my armour, went to speak to the king, and found him fully armed and sitting on a chair, with the good knights of his own division, also in full panoply of war, around him. I asked him if he wished me and my men to go and stand outside the camp, so as to prevent the Saracens from damaging our tents. On hearing my question, Jean de Beaumont called out to me at the top of his voice and commanded me, in the king's name, not to leave my quarters till his Majesty ordered me to do so.

During this time Gautier d'Autreche had got himself armed at all points in his pavilion. After mounting his horse, with his shield at his neck and his helmet on his head, he had the flaps of his pavilion lifted, and struck spurs into his horse to ride against the Turks. As he was going out of his pavilion, alone and unattended, all his men raised a loud cry and shouted 'Chatillon!' But it so happened that before he reached the Turks he fell; his horse leaped over his body and went careering forward, still covered with its master's arms, right into the midst of our enemies. This was because the Saracens, for the most part, were mounted on mares, and the stallion was consequently attracted to their side.

Those who watched the incident told us that four Turks came rushing towards my lord Gautier as he lay on the ground, and aimed great blows with their maces at his body as they went by. The Constable of France and several of the king's sergeants went and rescued him, and carried him

[1] Damietta – a town in Egypt

A battle, from a French manuscript of about A.D. 1240.

back in their arms to his pavilion. When he arrived there he could not speak. Several of the army surgeons and physicians went to see him, and because he did not seem to them to be in danger of dying they bled him in both arms.

Very late that night Aubert de Narcy said to me that we ought to go and look in on him, for as yet we had not seen him, and besides he was a man of high repute and great valour. As we entered his pavilion his chamberlain came forward to meet us and asked us to move quietly, so as not to wake his master. We found him lying on a coverlet of miniver; we went up to him very softly, and saw that he was dead. When the king was told of this he remarked that he would not care to have a thousand men like Gautier for they would want to go against his orders as this knight had done.

The Saracens came every night into our camp on foot, and killed our men where they found them sleeping. In this way they killed my lord

Courtenay's sentinel, and after cutting off his head and t~~~~ ~
them, left his body lying ~~~~~

~~~~~ ~ad been doing, the
~~~ future carry out this duty on foot. In consequence the whole camp was safely guarded by our men, who were
spread out in such a way that each man was within arm's length of
his neighbour.

From *The Life of Saint Louis* by JEAN DE JOINVILLE

For discussion

*Which details do you think could only have been recorded by someone who
was with the army at this time?*

What do you think of the treatment that the army doctors gave the knight?

*Do you agree with the King's comment on the knight's behaviour, or do you
sympathize with his eagerness to do battle with the Saracens?*

*Unlike the Anglo-Saxon leaders, crusading knights were not often killed in
battle because they were encased in strong armour, and mounted on big
war-horses, and most of all because it was more profitable to take them
prisoner and make their families pay a high ransom for them. Which of
these battle stories interests you most? Why?*

Questions of a Studious Working Man

Who built Thebes of the seven gates?
In the books you find the names of kings.
Was it the kings who hauled chunks of rocks
        to the place?
And Babylon, many times demolished,
Who raised it up again so many times? In
        what houses
Of gold-glittering Lima did the builders live?
Where, the evening that the Great Wall of China
        was finished,
Did the masons go? Great Rome
Is full of triumphal arches. Over whom
Did the Caesars triumph? Had Byzantium,
        much praised in song,
Only palaces for its inhabitants? Even in
        fabulous Atlantis
The very night the Ocean engulfed it,
The drowning still roared for their slaves.
Young Alexander conquered India.
Was it he alone?
Caesar defeated the Gauls.
Did he not have a cook at least in his service?
Philip of Spain wept when his armada
Had sunk. Was he the only one to weep?
Frederick the Second won the Seven Years War,
        Who
Else won that war?

Every page a victory.
Who cooked the feast for the victors?
Every ten years a great man.
Who paid the bill?
So many accounts
So many questions.   BERTOLT BRECHT

182

For writing

A book of tales of the not-so-distant past collected from grandparents and other old people.

A history of your area — town or parish.

A history of your school.

Individual family histories. These might include family trees, accounts of different cities or parts of England lived in, photographs, drawings of houses, maps, reminiscences, adventures, and romances where they are known and invented stories about the members of the family who are only names. It is also said that every family has its black sheep. Include some of these.

Interview some grown-ups who are willing to talk to you for a few minutes.

Collect some biographical details from them such as:
Where they were born and grew up.
First jobs.
Did they have a wild or a hard youth?
When did they settle down? Did they marry?
Present interests.
Which part of their lives they liked best.

Write a short biography of the person you have interviewed.

A History Lesson

Kings
like golden gleams
made with a mirror on the wall.

A non-alcoholic pope,
knights without arms,
arms without knights.

The dead like so many strained noodles,
a pound of those fallen in battle,
two ounces of those who were executed,

several heads
like so many potatoes
shaken into a cap –

empires rise and fall
at a wave of the pointer,
the blood is blotted out –

And only one small boy,
who was not paying the least attention,
will ask
between two victorious wars:

And did it hurt in those days too?

MIROSLAV HOLUB

Doing and Saying

play and practical activities — saying without doing — instructions — reports

A Japanese caligrapher.

...the world in eighty minutes.

'That isn't possible,' his grandmother told him, but he only grinned at her.

'The impossible is the most fun,' he said.

She went with him to the door of the old Wolf place. 'If you go that fast, you won't live to regret it,' she warned him, but he grinned again, showing a tongue as long as a necktie.

'That's an old wolves' tale,' he said, and went on his reckless way.

He bought a 1979 Blitzen Bearcat, a combination motorcar and air-plane, with skyrocket getaway, cyclone speedrive, cannonball takeoff, blindall headlights, magical retractable monowings, and lightning pushbutton transformationizer. 'How fast can this crate go without burning up?' he asked the Blitzen Bearcat salesman.

'I don't know,' the salesman said, 'but I have a feeling you'll find out.'

The wealthy young wolf smashed all the ground records and air records and a lot of other things in his trip around the world, which took him only 78.5 minutes from the time he knocked down the Washington Monument on his takeoff to the time he landed where it had stood. In the crowd that welcomed him home, consisting of about eleven creatures, for all the others were hiding under beds, there was a speed-crazy young wolfess, with built-in instantaneous pickup ability, and in no time at all the wolf and his new-found mate were setting new records for driving upside down, backward, blindfolded, handcuffed, and cockeyed, doubled, and redoubled.

One day, they decided to see if they could turn into Central Park from Fifth Avenue while travelling at a rate of 175 miles an hour, watching television, and holding hands. There was a tremendous shattering, crashing, splitting, roaring, blazing, cracking, and smashing, ending in a fiery display of wheels, stars, cornices, roofs, treetops, glass, steel, and people, and it seemed to those spectators who did not die of seizures as they watched, that great red portals opened in the sky, swinging inward on mighty hinges, revealing an endless nowhere, and then closed behind the flying and flaming wolves with a clanking to end all clanking, as if those gates which we have been assured shall not prevail had, in fact, prevailed.

Moral: Where most of us end up there is no knowing, but the hellbent get where they are going.

From *Vintage Thurber* by JAMES THURBER

(a) *Try out some improvised dramatic versions of this story. You will probably need to use quite a lot of mime for parts of it.*

(b) *Rewrite this story as a play.*

For discussion *before you write. Study the instructions in Appendix 7, page 232 to see how to set out a play.*

You need not confine your characters' talk to the things they say in the story. You should turn some of the description (and narrative) into speech. For example, can you turn the statement that the 'speed-crazy young wolfess had a built-in instantaneous pickup ability' into dialogue, or their plan to try to turn a corner while travelling at 175 miles per hour, watching television and holding hands?

How much of this story can you get into dialogue and action?

There isn't much dialogue in the story. What proportion of action to speech are you going to have?

Do the characters show what kind of people they are in their speech? In their actions? Or in both?

How are you going to make this play end so that it is clear to the audience? Shall you just write 'curtain' in its stage directions, or can you do more than this?

188

...saying than doing. Which version did you find more enjoyable to watch?

Think of some of the things you do with other people during the day (apart from lessons) and consider whether you talk as you perform these operations.

For instance:

> *Shopping.*
> *Playing chess or draughts.*
> *Taking photographs.*
> *Washing up.*
> *Cleaning a bicycle.*
> *Playing playground games.*
> *Making a dress.*
> *Operating a tape-recorder.*
> *Planing a piece of wood.*
> *Learning to ride a bicycle or swim.*
> *Performing a conjuring trick.*

Is the talk part of what you do or not?

Do you talk about it before you start?

Do you talk about it afterwards?

Now consider school-work.

How much talk do you need before and during your homework?

How much talk do you need when you have had your work back?

In what ways are 'doing lessons' different from or like doing the things in the list above?

In the days when all work was done by hand a common way of *using language to help* was by work songs. There were different shanties for most of the laborious joint operations on big sailing ships; there were also spinning songs, ploughing songs, and many others.

Here is a children's game which is half action and half song.

Poor Jenny is A-Weeping

The children stand in a ring with one girl in the middle and they sing:

Poor Jenny is a-weeping, a-weeping, a-weeping,
Poor Jenny is a-weeping on a bright summer day.
Pray tell us what you're weeping for, a-weeping for, a-weeping for,
Pray tell us what you're weeping for on a bright summer day.

The girl in the centre of the ring must answer:

In and out the window,
In and out the window,
In and out the window
As you have done before.

Then the other children sing:

Stand and face your lover,
Stand and face your lover,
Stand and face your lover
As you have done before.

The girl in the middle then points at a boy in the ring and all the children sing:

Chase him all round Dublin,
Chase him all round Dublin,
Chase him all round Dublin
As you have done before.

Then the chase begins, in and out the ring, till he is caught. Then it is someone else's turn.

If you were playing this game and not just reading about it, you would be doing things as soon as each verse of the song was ended.

190

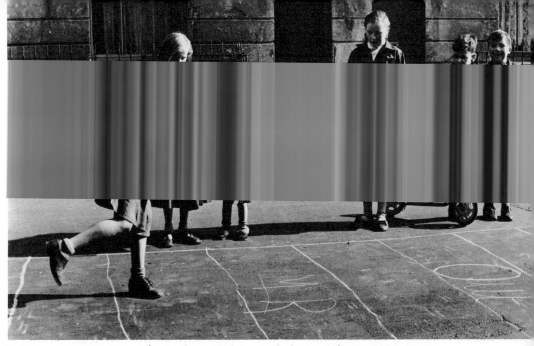

Think of something you have done which needed more than one person to do it, and write it up in the form of a dialogue. That is, you only write down the actual words used. (See Appendix 7, page 232)

Suggestions:

A game of cards or chess.

Working on a ladder.

Getting a dinghy alongside and made fast.

Improvising a play.

Pitching a tent.

Preparing a room for a party.

Helping someone to get out of a room with a jammed lock.

Helping someone saw off a branch of a high tree.

Any other operation you have taken part in.

Discuss *how much the words tell you about what is happening.*

Note. If you have a tape-recorder available and put it on and forget about it while a group is doing something together such as playing a game of cards or improvising a play or planning some expedition, you would then have a record of the words actually used *as part of the job.* You may also have language used that is not part of the job, for example, gossip or jokes on the side.

saying without doing — instructions

When you want to tell (instruct) someone how to play a game, or take a photograph, or work a tape-recorder it is very difficult unless you can perform the actions with the object itself. It is difficult because the words and the actions are real partners and neither is very effective without the other. This is why printed instructions that go with anything you buy are often difficult to understand and remember until you have carried out the operation. How much sense do the following instructions make for you if you read them without performing the operation?

Threading the Tape

Prior to threading the tape pull the two rotatable upper parts of the spindles and twist them until they reach a position relative to the fixed lower parts as shown. Place a full reel on the left hand turntable and an empty reel on the right hand turntable. Unwind approximately 10 inches of tape which causes the full reel to rotate anticlockwise. Hold the free end of the tape taut, as shown, and insert it vertically into the tape slot. Then pass the free end of the tape upwards through the threading slot in the upper flange of the empty reel, so that approximately 0·4 inches of tape emerge above the reel. Rotate the empty reel anticlockwise for slightly more than one turn.

From *Operating Instructions. Uher 8000*

Instructions (or directions) point forwards — towards the future. They are, as it were, commands, which tell you what to do next, but they can only be given by someone who has performed the actions already and knows what happened at each stage. So they are, in fact, worked out *after* the things have been done.

Therefore, the easiest way to learn to give instructions is to begin by *reporting how you did something*. Reports look backwards to what has happened and they are easier to write than instructions because you have the memory of what you actually did to help you.

saying without doing — reports

on the Grawnshee; an' I'll be last in both for the sake of the game.'

Then they all laid their caps in a row at an angle against the wall of a house. They took turns, Touhy first, and Johnny last, trying to roll a ball into one of the caps, the player doing his best to avoid rolling it into his own. When the ball rolled into a cap, the rest scattering in flight, caught the ball up, and flung it at a boy nearest and easiest to hit. If he missed a pebble was put in his cap, but if he hit a boy, then a pebble was put in the cap of the boy the ball had struck. The game went on till a boy had six pebbles or more (the number being decided at the beginning of the game). Then the boy with the six pebbles in his cap had to stand by the wall, and stretch out his arm, and press the back of his hand firm against the bricks. Then each boy, with a hard, half-solid ball, had six shots at the outstretched hand; each aiming at hitting it as hard as he could, and enjoying the start of pain appearing on a boy's face whenever the hard ball crashed into the palm of his hand. Each boy had to go through the ordeal, the number of blows being the same as the number of pebbles in his cap.

Johnny liked the ordeal; his hands were small and firm and hard, and the impact of the ball stung his hand far less than it stung the softer and larger hands of his comrades. So the game went on till they were tired, and many eyes were blinking back the tears from the smart of hands that were red, and stung fiercely.

From *I Knock at the Door* by SEAN O'CASEY

And here is a report by a 12-year-old boy of how he first operated his 'Scalextric' set.

Scalextric Set

The set comprised two cars, a red Lotus and a blue Cooper, curved and straight track pieces, a chicane which was where the two tracks almost met, six crash barriers, ten green banking wedges, twelve oil drums, twelve straw bale obstacles, and two red and black hand throttles which controlled the speed of the two cars.

It was a wonderful feeling putting the cars on the track for the very first time. I felt very proud. Everything smelt new and clean and my sister and my cousin were quarreling who was to have first go. I picked up a hand throttle and pressed. The car went speeding off into the first bend and crashed. I placed it back on the track and started off again. I knew now that much care and skill were needed to keep the car on the track in a fast race. I slowed down the car when it got to the next bend, then after passing that speeded up along the straight. I was soon challenged to a race by my sister and immediately consented.

KENNETH

1. *Write a report of how you did any of the things suggested in the lists on pages 189 and 191, or any other thing that you prefer to write about. Think before you begin to write of the exact order in which you did things. Then write it down, step by step, using the past tense.*

For discussion

Read your report aloud and let other people who are familiar with what you have written about check your account of it. You may need to amend it when you have discussed it with them.

2. *Write an account of how you first learned to do something, such as swimming, riding a bicycle, skating, making a cake, etc.*

Here is an account by a boy of how he learned to ride a bicycle

...began as soon as Jim got the bright blue bicycle out of his black broken-down shed. He then helped me to get on to the bicycle's saddle because it was a bit high then I jumped down while he held the bicycle to steady it then he said try getting on it without any help. I did as he asked without any trouble because Jim was holding the bicycle. I was very eager to start riding but I knew this lesson was important.

Jim then told me that the best way to get on a bicycle is to push it a bit then put the right foot on the right pedal while your left foot is scooting, then quickly cock the left leg over the saddle, then place it on the left pedal and you would automatically sit on the saddle and start pedalling round and round. I tried doing this at first with Jim holding the bicycle up. Then I began practising the way he had told me. He said he would be a few feet away to hold the bicycle, also to help me off. After a few days I had mastered this, then came the next stage, riding and balancing.

Jim told me next that it was easier to balance on a bicycle if you move fast but the faster you go the more careful you must be. He then said he would be at the back of the bicycle holding it and running with me all the time. I started off the way I had been taught and pedalled along. It seemed very easy but I wasn't really balancing for Jim was balancing me. When I got near to the end of the alley Jim shouted to me, 'put the brakes on'. I did so and I soon came to a halt. The bicycle was falling, so I got off the saddle and put my feet on the ground. This stopped myself falling over but my socks got black and greasy by getting in contact with the oily chain.

I went up and down the alley several times, then the next day after a few more rides, as I was riding along down the alley I could hear Jim's running feet behind me but for no reason at all. I glanced round and I saw Jim hurriedly, as I was looking, clutching onto the back. I braked hard and got off and asked Jim if he had done it before and if he didn't hold at all. He answered yes except when I unbalanced then he'd steadied me. I exclaimed 'then I can do it. I can ride a bicycle!'

Jim interrupted me, 'I know but you won't have the confidence of me being near to help you, and stopping is one thing that I can't teach you,' he had said.

I picked up the technique of stopping, after my mum and dad bought me a bicycle, so that I could practise a lot more.

I had learnt how to ride a bicycle, if not properly, and as I got older I began riding on the roads.   KENNETH

Discussion

.... *using words.*

3. *Write out a set of instructions for learning to ride a bicycle — excluding everything in the way of a story.*

The form of the verb for instructions is called 'the Imperative'. It will be quite familiar to you because children hear a lot of instructions!

Examples: 'do this', 'take that', 'hold this', 'put this in that place', etc. (See Appendix 7, page 235).

So, use the imperative, i.e., tell your readers what to do (or not to do).

Take a new line for each instruction.

When you have finished check it with a friend.

4. *Write another set of instructions for doing something else, for example, performing a card trick or a conjuring trick, frying an egg, threading a needle, threading a tape-recorder.*

Here is a report of all sorts of things happening together:

Life in our Kitchen

It is Sunday morning once again. Although this day is supposed to be a day of rest it is a day of chaos. Let me describe a typical Sunday in our house.

The first person to get up is Dad. He gets my mum and me a cup of tea. After about half an hour we get up. It is still quiet in the house. My mum starts to get clean clothes ready for my three brothers when they get up. I sit and read the papers. We always dress and eat in the kitchen first thing in the morning; it's warmer in there. Everything is still quiet. Suddenly there is a loud bang followed by a scream, then another, and yet another. My three brothers have just got up. They come tearing down the stairs two and three at a time. Even Stevie who is only four. Bump! Into the kitchen they rush and down goes the clothes-horse with all the clean washing on it. Mum isn't pleased.

After everyone has finished putting the blame on to someone else they all sit down to the table, still clad in pyjamas, to eat breakfast. We usually have eggs and bacon on Sundays but Stevie usually wants fried bread, after mum has cooked him an egg. Dad sits down and is just going to enjoy a mouthful of egg when jab! his fork is pushed half-way down his throat. Freddie is trying to get to the other side of the table. About ten minutes later the three horrors are still playing about but they decide to eat their breakfast. Of course it is cold by then but mum makes sure they eat it.

When breakfast is finished the table is cleared. At least my mum and I have a good try to clear it. My brothers seem to be everywhere, playing cowboys with the rolling pin or swimming the channel with mum's best pillows from the living room. There is complete chaos. But then my mother folds up the table to reveal our bath. Then there is silence. And then another cowboy game. This time the one who gets killed first has to be put in the river to drown, the river being the bath. Jimmy, my eldest brother slips and falls to the floor. Of course he can't let my young brother, Freddie get the better of him so up he gets and lands Freddie a blow across the ear but my dad comes in and soon one of them lands up in the bath. All the time its drawing near to eleven o'clock and that is the time for them to go to church. They wouldn't miss church because each summer there is an outing to the seaside. At last Jimmy and Freddie are out of the way but we are still left with Stevie. Mum usually leaves him in the bath. I make the cakes for tea and usually we have visitors.

Everything is ready on the table and I put my apron on. I mix the dough and put the currants in. Then, just as I go to put the jam in, a small hand slithers on to the table and takes a large lump of the dough.

Smack! That puts a stop to his games. Well

...once more. The plates are set out for dinner and the potatoes are browning nicely.

At twelve o'clock my brothers come in. They fling their coats on chairs and get out books and toys. Everyone gets the humps and dinner seems to have stopped cooking. We usually have our dinner at two, but to get it done in our house you need to start doing it at about seven o'clock in the morning. But when we go into the dining room to have dinner the kitchen is clean and quiet once more. It is my brothers' job to clear away the things from the table on Sundays. They do it quite well. And my mum and dad and myself stay in the dining room for a while.

At three o'clock my mum and I go into the kitchen to do the washing up. Washing up! It needs a good spring clean. Oh yes. My brothers have cleared the table all right. They have stood the plates one on top of the other without throwing away the leavings, and the consequence is that the gravy and bits of potatoes and greens have fallen all over the table. Well, they did try to help. But all I can say is that whoever said that Sunday was a day of rest ought to try and spend it at our house.

PEGGY

1. *All sorts of things are going on at the same time here. Children and grown-ups doing things separately or together, getting in each other's way and yet getting things done.*

Choose a place and a time when a lot of people are busy doing things and write an account of what is going on. This time use the present tense, as if you were there. (See Appendix 7, page 235).

Some suggestions (which you need not take.)
   A railway station.
   A market.
   A party.
   A barber's or hairdresser's shop.
   A crowded beach in summer.
   School Sports' Day.
   The woodwork or metalwork shop at school.

2. *Select from your busy scene a single operation performed by one person and describe exactly what was done. This time use the past tense. (See Appendix 7, page 235).*

Consider how successful Henry has been in the following description.

Using a Plane

Before planing make sure your bench is clear except for the tools needed for your particular job, and make sure the wood is firmly set in the vice. When sharpening the plane, remove the cutter and unscrew the back of it. You will see the edge is roughly ground. Hold it with the level flat on the oil stone and then raise the hand slightly so that the edge alone touches. Work it to and fro until a burr can be detected when the thumb is drawn across the back of the cutter. Now reverse the cutter, holding it this time flat and rub it once or twice until the burr is removed. Finally strop both sides on a piece of leather. If there is a line of white the cutter is still blunt for a sharp edge is invisible . . .

When all the preparation is done, we can get down to the more pleasant side of planing. The right hand should firmly grasp the handle of the plane, and the fingers of the left hand should curl underneath with the thumb pressing down to guide it. When beginning the cut exert pressure on the front of the plane, and as the far end is reached, transfer it to the rear. Then after this process, the plane will really begin to move. I love to listen to it singing over the wood and throwing

out flowers of curled-up shavings. The rhythmical
of the ist

, you follow what is happening?

If you think it could be improved, how would you amend it?

Is it in the form of instructions or report, or both?

How important are the last six lines?

Is it better or worse than the piece you have written yourself on doing some particular thing? In what ways is it better, or worse than your own?

APPENDIX 1

The bones of a story
Chapters and paragraphs
'I' or 'he'
Conversation

1. *The bones of a story*

A skeleton isn't at all like the creature whose bones it is, and the bones of a story are not at all like the story itself. *Do you recognise the following 'skeleton'?*

A boat load of young men set out to steal some gold. They got away with a princess as well as the gold and a great chase followed.

But no one would think this much of a story. It needs flesh and blood and breath and speech before it comes alive and makes you listen to it.
Are your stories starved, boney things, or do they stand up and shout? Here is a 'starved' bit of a story:

At the foot of a tree was a big snake. It hissed loudly but Medea spoke a spell and sprinkled magic to make it go to sleep, and Jason grabbed the fleece and ran off with it.

Some of John Rattenbury's story is rather thin and boney; for instance he writes:

The same day, my wife, having heard of my situation, with some other females, the wives of my companions, came on board. Our interview was short; but long enough for me to entreat her to get a good boat and come off for me the next morning. In the evening, I opened part of my plan to my companions; and desired them to be prepared to act according to the hints I had given them.

See if you can expand this bit of his story so that it is as alive and exciting as the account of the escape from the brig Catherine *which comes next. Ask yourself questions of this sort:*
How did his wife hear that he was a prisoner on board the Catherine?

Who might have told her?

*............ ...... present at the interview? His fellow
smugglers or members of the ship's crew or officers? How did he convey
his plan to her? and so on.*

*Now write up this part of the story as fully as you can. Try to make it a story
in itself within the full story of his capture and escape from the* Catherine.

2. Chapters and paragraphs

A good story is always fairly long and has a lot of detail.

But it is not easy to find your way around, either in writing it or in
reading it without some signposts.

*Chapter headings are signposts in a story. Try dividing John Rattenbury's
story (or Jason and the Golden Fleece) into three or four chapters with titles.*

*Paragraphs are smaller signposts in between the larger ones which are
chapters. Both show a change of direction in the story. Someone new
arrives, or a different bit of the adventure begins.*

*You decide for yourself where you want paragraphs to come, though most
people make these breaks when they change course, as it were, and begin
something a bit different. Sometimes writers make a new paragraph just
because they have written a whole page without one and it is easier to read
something which has a few pauses while you get your breath!*

*You show a new paragraph by putting a full stop at the end of the sentence
you have just finished and by starting the next one on the line below,
a bit in from the margin, like this:*

We put in at a promontory called Bob's Nose; my companions jumped
out; I was the last man, having steered the boat, and as I was in the act

of doing so, a shot passed close to my head, but it did not touch me.
As soon as I got on shore, I scrambled up the cliffs; . . . etc.

3. *Position of the writer. 'I' or 'he'*

In reminiscences writers use the first person 'I'. It is their story and they tell it as they remember it.

In fiction a writer can put himself in the position of the character who is supposed to be telling the story and write in the first person as 'I'; or he can put himself in the position of a spectator and write in the third person, 'he' or 'she' or 'they'.

A real spectator, of course, doesn't know what people are thinking and feeling, whereas a writer in the position of a spectator often imagines himself into the heads of his characters and says what they might be thinking and feeling, for instance the story-writer says about Medea:

Medea's heart was filled with agonizing fears. . . . She realized at once that her father could not fail to know what she had done for Jason, ... She also feared the maids who had seen something of their secret meeting.

(a) *Rewrite the story of Jason as if you were Jason, and use 'I'.*

(b) *Rewrite part of John Rattenbury's story as if you were the second mate telling the story; use 'he' about John Rattenbury.*

4. *Conversation*

Most people like conversation in a story, but if there is too much conversation, there won't be much story.

Which of the five stories in this section has most conversation?

If a story is mostly conversation do you need paragraphs?

Look at the stories printed here and notice how conversation is set out on the page by the printer.

Make a set of rules for setting out conversation on a page.

Be sure to include rules about:

1. *Quotation marks.*
2. *Paragraphs or starting on a fresh line.*

2. *How remarks by th* ......

......

...... of the third person, or write a play.

APPENDIX 2

Youth Hostels Association
Maps
Description
Notes and lists

1. Youth Hostels Association

Hotels, hostels, and inns have signs hanging over their doors or from a post on the road outside with their names on them and a picture of their names.

The triangle with the letters Y.H.A. is the sign of the Youth Hostels Association. You may notice it sticking out of a hedge in a country lane with an arrow pointing to what looks like a farmhouse or in front of an old mill or a row of quarry-workers' cottages on the edge of the sea.

To stay at a youth hostel you must be a member of the Y.H.A. and have your membership card with you. It costs only a few shillings to join, and you must be over five years old! There is no upper limit for age, so grandparents are not excluded but you need to be active to be a member because you may not arrive in any kind of power vehicle, only on foot, by bicycle or by canoe.

To stay the night costs very little and you may buy a meal at the hostel or cook your own in the hostel kitchen, but in return you have to clear up after your efforts and do about half an hour's work to help the warden, such as peeling potatoes, washing up, or sweeping the bunk rooms.

The hostels are dotted about all over Great Britain (and Europe and North America too) in all the wildest and most interesting parts. The handbook of the Youth Hostels Association gives a map of where they all are and how many miles apart and a great deal of other information for people who want to explore England and haven't much money. Their headquarters address is: 29 John Adam Street, London, W.C.2.

2. Maps

The oldest maps were pictorial ones; they tried to show what an area looked like and contained written notes about events and drawings of animals, winds, trees, etc.

208

Modern maps are really diagrammatic codes; you have to know the code to be able to read them. Ord~

~ and discuss whether

~g a map, or writing, or thinking – or all of these.

What is being related to what in this poem?

3. Description

Except for scientific purposes (and school exercises!) no one writes description just for itself. *It is a kind of tool for doing something else.*

(a) You need it for writing stories (fiction or true ones)

Without enough description you get the bald writing referred to in Appendix I; with too much description you will bore your readers and make them lose the drift of the story.

(b) You need it for recording exactly what things are like

Description is of great importance to explorers of all kinds. What has not been discovered before must be described and related to things we already know. In a sense everyone seeing things for the first time is an explorer and this is true both of the explorations you do on your own out of school and of the work you do in school.

Some occasions for describing
Select what you put in to please yourself.
   A fire engine going down the street.
   A plane landing.
   Going out from a warm room on a cold night.
   A street corner.
   An embarrassing incident.
   Your front door.

O

A toad (if you have ever seen one).
The palm of your left hand.
Anything else you would be interested to describe.
A building that is being demolished.
Ploughing.
A farmyard.
A zoo animal.

Exact descriptions required.

Something you have made — any thing.
  A piece of apparatus you have used in school.
  The route from your house to the station.

Two things in order to distinguish them from each other, for example, two kinds of dog, or two makes of car, or wheat and barley, turnips and swedes, a steam and a diesel electric train, a traffic warden and a children's crossing warden etc.

4. Notes and lists

Explorers use all sorts of records in which they describe their discoveries — diaries, notes, lists, maps, diagrams, and they record very different kinds of things.

(a) Lists

The writer of the Cornish diary on page 57 lists the birds and animals seen in the area and gives a brief description of their appearance in note form.

In school, in Geography particularly, one often makes lists to record places, physical features of the country, products and processes and these often include brief descriptions.

This kind of record is very different from a story and needs to be set down in a different way. It is a kind of summary and leaves out many details of explanation that would be in a story. It is therefore important to set it out in a different way, so that it can be easily read and understood. A list should be set out down the page, each new item exactly underneath the one before. The descriptions should not be ~~~~ ~ with the items in the list

there are some suggestions for practice work on this kind of record.

Places visited outside your home area.

Kinds of trees growing in your area.

Objects found on the tideline of a beach; classify them in your arrangement.

Things to take in your suitcase for a summer holiday abroad.

Old buildings.

Birds and animals.

Curiosities.

Things sold in local market.

Physical features of your neighbourhood (rivers, hills, crops, woods, streets, public buildings, parks, swimming baths, etc.)

(b) Notes

Notes are reminders.

Like lists, they are only useful if you can read them quickly and they do, in fact, *remind* you.

Therefore they must be legible, neat and not look as if they are a page from a story!

Use spaces and fresh lines to separate notes on different subjects, and use numbers and capital letters.

Here is a page from a boy's Geography notebook. It contains a list and a set of notes.

Discuss the information contained in the way it is set out.

Ways of obtaining a living in the Highlands

Forestry commission	Shepherding
Farming	Weaving
Fishing	Spinning
Ferrying	Thatching
Game keeping	Bus driving
Highland pony dealing	Shop keeping etc.
Raising Highland cattle	Whisky making
Making aluminium	Hydro-electric power

Fibres to Fabrics

Where from	How obtained
Wool – from Australia, New Zealand (and sheep)	The fibres are sheared from the sheep in one piece. It is then carded and spun into thread.
Silk – comes from silk worms or caterpillars. They feed on mulberry leaves in a warm climate.	It is taken from the cocoon of the caterpillar and spun out like wool, but it is finer and smoother.
Cotton – comes from sub-tropical lands like America. It has a white flower and is found in 'bolls'.	When taken from the 'bolls' it is carded and spun like other fibres.

Is this a 'map'?

If not, what is it? It certainly isn't a story or an article.

What further information is given by the arrangement into six 'cells'?

Rewrite it as a piece of continuous informational prose, such as you might find in a Geography text-book.

Compare the two versions.

212

APPENDIX 3

, ..., sometimes as collections on their own, sometimes in books also containing work by professional writers.[1] Plays, stories, and poems by young people can be heard from time to time on some of the B.B.C. programmes, and many schools produce duplicated magazines in addition to the printed one. Also, exhibitions and 'pin-ups' are on the increase. In many schools one can see Wall Magazines, or exhibitions of field studies in Geography or History, or records of school journeys. Pupils are also beginning to make films, and all these practical things involve various kinds of writing which will be read by other people.

The upshot of all this is that pupils need to be able to look after their own work; they can't rely on teachers to do all the revision (or correcting) for them.

This section is designed to help pupils who want to get work ready to be seen by 'The Public'! The Public, of course, may be the members of one class, or of a year group, or the school, or the real Public, i.e. anyone who sees what is exhibited whether it is by chance or by special invitation.

(a) Revising your own work: is that what you wanted to say?

Words are rather like young children; they like to arrange themselves. They come tumbling out in their own order — or they won't come at all — and sometimes, when they have come, they interrupt you by saying things you didn't intend, or by saying only half of what you wanted them to say.

So, the first job is to read through what you have written — or read it to a friend — and ask yourself: 'Is that what I wanted to say?' If it isn't, start again, or alter what you have written, but it is often better and more interesting to start again.

[1]Young Writers, Young Readers. Ed. Ford.   Hutchinson
Poems by Children   Ed. Baldwin   Routledge & Kegan Paul
Every Man will Shout   Ed. Mansfield.   Oxford University Press

Here are five attempts to write about a stream by a girl of 12 who wrote during her holidays. She tries it as a poem and in prose.
What do you think it was that she wanted to say, and that kept escaping her?

April 2nd. *The Stream*

It starts up high above,
Up in a mountain bare.
First it slowly trickles,   Not how I want
To its own merry tune.   it to be.
Then it falls swiftly,
Over granit boulders.

April 3rd. *The Stream*

In a mountain bare,
It starts from a spring.
Bub-uling, Bub-uling,
Down the mountain.   Lines wrong length.
When it reach/es,
The bottom,
It dor/dals along.

April 3rd. *The Stream*

Close to the sun,
On a mountain bare,
That's where my poem begins.

Down it falls,
Down to a meadow green,
That's where my poem is best.

It trickles along.
To join the river wide,
That's where my poem's in company.

214

and ended in the sea, you would see many interesting and beautiful things:
At. . . (to be continued)

April 4th.   *Continuation of 'The Stream'*

At the top the stream goes bubbling over heather covered rocks. About
a mile before the valley the stream forms a wonderful and magnificent
waterfall. The noise is deafening and within ten. . . .

(to be continued)

ANNA

What changes does she make in the different versions?
*What different things is she trying to get down on paper in the different
attempts?*
Do you prefer the prose ones or the poems?
*She herself seems surprised by one of them; what is different about this
one?*

(b) Revising for the duplicator, or the printer: making a fair copy

Reading a manuscript is often a difficult job, even for the person who wrote
it! Writing is laborious; pens leak and blot; spelling is often guesswork, and
punctuation isn't necessary for the writer – but it is essential for the *reader*.
So when you are writing and concentrating on trying to make words obey
you, handwriting, spelling, and punctuation are usually forgotten. This is
quite natural, because you are writing, and you don't need them in any very
perfect form at this stage, but when you have written your piece and have
revised what it says so that you are satisfied with it, then you will want to

show it to someone else. This may be your teacher, or you may be writing something for a wider audience such as a form folder of writings, or a wall magazine, or for some joint work with other people which is to go up on a wall somewhere, or for a duplicated or printed magazine.

Now, it becomes important for you to *switch your attention* from being a writer to being a *reader*. This means you now have the job of correcting the errors in the written symbols that represent your words, so you need to make a 'fair copy'.

Handwriting and layout

This needs to be as clear as you can make it. Paragraphs, underlinings, and capital letters all help – and spaces too. The actual arrangement, the way your work is set out on the page, will help or hinder your readers in understanding what you have written. Newspapers know all about this, and it is worth looking at some papers to see how they do this job of 'layout', i.e. arrangement on the page.

Spelling and punctuation

The fact is that almost no-one can spell perfectly, so all you can do is to revise your work as best you can and make a fair copy which probably won't be perfect, but it will be near enough. Dictionaries and other people will help you to get your spelling right enough; punctuation is more difficult. You need to make it as sensible as you can, and gradually learn how the various signs are used. Look at printed books and newspapers to see how they use the various stops, and remember that *the whole point of it is to help the reader.*

Usually, errors in spelling and punctuation are not bad enough to prevent people from understanding what you have written; they merely make people laugh, and distract their attention from the story or poem or whatever has been written, but sometimes they are so bad that the reader completely fails to make sense of what is on the page.

Discuss the following piece of writing from this point of view: Can you read it? It is a genuine piece of writing by a schoolboy and his handwriting was perfectly legible.

A Town at Night

..... and gicus sers ben nigth is so go thea erur barss wanet to gierr in and has som Foren all the world is at wor at nigth. . . .

BARRY

2. Proof reading

Suggestions

1. *Use the printer's proof-reading sheet on page 239 to correct one of your manuscripts. Take a short one to start on.*

2. *Make an error count of all the errors you can find in the last piece of writing you did. Keep a record at the back of your English book and see whether your error 'temperature' goes up or down over the term's work. It is helpful to record the date, title, and the number of errors in the form of a chart, and just fill it in each time you do a new piece of work. If you want to keep an eye on your spelling, you can have two columns (or three) for the errors – like this:*

Date	Title	Spelling mistakes	Punctuation mistakes	Other mistakes	Total
4 Dec. 1968	My Brothers	15	7	4	26
1 May 1969	Landing on Mars	5	7	5	17

...and so on.

Since the longer pieces will naturally tend to have more mistakes in them, and since, as you get older you are likely to use more ambitious words, the figure for the *total* number of errors may be misleading, but if you count the number of mistakes per page you will have a rough guide as to how your spelling or your punctuation is getting on.

3. *English and Biology*

Personal writing
Impersonal writing
Notes

When you write like the boy did about his racing pigeons on page 96 you write to please yourself, exactly as *you* want it; this is personal writing. Stories and poems also are personal writing.

But sometimes you need to exclude the personal viewpoint and write for everyone in a voice that does not therefore belong to anyone in particular. This is *impersonal* writing, used for most scientific articles, reports, observations, and notes. The first person, 'I', is seldom used, and instead of 'you' it is usual to write the more impersonal (and rather clumsy) 'one', for example, instead of '*You* soon get used to it' which is like speech, scientific notes would say '*one* soon gets used to it'.

Here are several sets of notes on lessons.
Read them carefully and discuss their value as notes. (What are notes for?)
Incidentally, which of these do you find most interesting, and/or useful?

(*a*) It was Biology after break and as usual we lined up outside the Biology room door. Miss Thompson was waiting outside with us as the last of us slipped into line. Miss Thompson had her arms folded, she always had her arms folded when we stood outside waiting; she usually gives us a lecture on how bad we are and we go in. There was some young man waiting for us, another student; this one seemed frightened, maybe that's why he chose birds as a subject to teach on. He spoke in broken sentences and couldn't wait to start writing; that wasn't much better and there was quite a lot of it on the board....

After break we marched slowly to technical drawing which is taken by Mr Day, a short man who always looks smart and might bite your head off if you ask him any questions. There are two more boys in our all-boy technical drawing class than in any other class so another boy and I must stand at the front until every boy is seated, and if any boy is absent one of us is allowed to work with the others. Today we both got a seat and I

And then he told us to make two holes in it and put it over the tube when
we had done this.

He put a chemical that we used last time into the water. And the water
was red and then we lit it and my one was rising and I thought this was
fascinating.

We call this expanding and it was rising higher and higher.

GEORGE

(c) The caterpillar feeds by holding the leaf in its legs and using its
mandibles in scissor-fashion. It eats through a terrific amount. The
caterpillar feeds on the plant on which its egg was laid.

It eats during its six weeks of life so naturally there must be some
expansion somewhere. This results in shedding its skin five times.

The caterpillar moves not unlike the worm in a concertina-like fashion,
gripping the surface with its posterior suckers while it stretches forward
with the rest of the body. Then the front suckers place themselves down
on the leaf and the rest of the body draws up.

BRIAN

Simon's notes on his Biology and Technical Drawing lessons are entirely his
own business. No one can say he ought to have put in anything other than he
did – what he observes and comments on are true *for him* but not necessarily
true for other people – but George's and Brian's have a very different
purpose.

How good are they as records that are generally true, i.e. true for everyone?
Can you follow what they say happens?
What are they for?
If to remind the writer, they may be satisfactory, but they leave rather a lot
to his memory.

If they are intended as an exact record then it looks as if they have left out some important things, for example, what was the chemical that turned the water red? Was the water in the flask or the tube? Where was the tube in relation to the flask? Was it the paper or the liquid that they lit? Again Brain is not precise enough. Does he mean the caterpillar laid an egg on the actual plant it feeds on, or that the egg it came out of is laid on the kind of plant on which it subsequently feeds. Furthermore he refers to its legs in paragraph 1 and its suckers in paragraph 3. Are these the same — or has it both legs and suckers?

Later on Brian writes up and expands his notes on the earthworm and produces a much more precise account of how the worm moves.

(*d*) The body of the earthworm contains a number of muscles which run down the whole length of the body. When the worm wants to move forward the muscles expand and allow the earthworm to stretch its body. Then the muscles contract and the hind end of the body is pulled up to the front. (Expansion and Contraction) On each segment of the earthworm's body there are four pair of bristles. When the worm is moving forward the bristles are withdrawn into the body. Then when the worm stops the bristles are put out and grip the surface of the soil so that if the worm is climbing up its burrow the bristles will stop it falling back.

This is good straight forward impersonal writing (description) and it can be checked by observation.

A **Fact** is something which is *generally* true. Science and History are about things that are generally true. Other kinds of writing such as stories, poems, and plays are about things as they *seem* to be, as *one* person sees them, and that person is the writer.

Fiction stories are not concerned with being true to facts, but *good stories* are concerned to be true to how people feel and think and behave in situations that are like life but are not true in fact. That is they are *personally* true.

So scientific writers are careful to distinguish between facts and their judgements (or opinions); that is between what is generally true and what is personally true.

(a) *Consider the kinds of truth to be found in:*

The reports about the Loch Ness Monster.
Darwin's journal.
The observations about the robin.
Sir Arthur Conan Doyle's story about the Lost World.
The Anglo-Saxon poem about Grendel.
Science fiction stories.

(b) *Consider what kind of truth you are concerned with in the writing you do in English, Science, and History.*

2. Classification

Everyone who has ever collected anything knows that collections have to be arranged in some sort of groups, for example, stamps, shells, plants, photographs, etc.

The arrangement you make fits the facts, as you know them – for example, stamps are usually grouped according to the countries they come from, and shells and plants are arranged by family. If you have a number of objects that you can't account for, you can't arrange (classify) them scientifically until you make a guess based on observation which relates them to the objects you already have or know about.

Practical exercises

Next time you go to a supermarket study the arrangement of the goods on the stands. What things are at eye level and hand level? What things are less easy to see? Can you think of a theory to explain the facts that you find? Check it by observation.

Partings

What do people say when they go away from each other? It is unusual (considered rather impolite) to get up and go away without saying anything.

Make a list of all the expressions you use, or have heard people use when they depart.

Here are some to begin with; can you add to this list?

> *Goodbye.*
> *Bye bye*
> *Bye.*
> *Bye then.*
> *Cheerio.*
> *See you.*
> *Be seeing you.*
> *Mind your step!*
> *Farewell.*
> *Be good.*

Classify (arrange) these in some way; i.e. find a theory which shows you how to group them. (Two groups? or four . . . ?)

Here are some suggestions to start you thinking:

> *That people of different ages use these different expressions;*

Irritable question: Why use technical terms? Why not a word everyone knows?

Why not indeed if you are writing for everyone.

The only time when there is any point in using technical terms is when you are writing as an expert for experts.

Re-read the passage on page 200 called 'Using a Plane'. Clearly this boy assumed that his reader knew as much as he did about using a plane and he was writing as an expert. So was Darwin in his journal of his explorations in South America.

Another irritable question: So experts use technical terms just to show they are experts? Snobs!

Not at all. Many technical terms have hidden meanings which an expert understands at once. For instance, you might describe a snake as being like a large earthworm in appearance but if you said "it is a vertebrate and an earthworm is an invertebrate", anyone who knows the classification of living creatures at once knows that however much it looks like a large worm it is different in all sorts of ways from animals without backbones. Again if you use the word 'mammal' to describe a whale, anyone who knows the meaning of mammal knows that it is not a fish, that its young are not hatched from eggs, that its breathing apparatus will be that of mammal and not a fish, and so on.

In short, when you use technical terms you are saying something about the ways in which things or ideas are related to each other, and most ordinary words don't do this.

Warning. It is only when you want to be very precise and scientific that you need to be technical – people who use technical language unnecessarily are terrible bores.

4. *Dictionaries*

A large dictionary which gives the derivation of words will show you the layers of meaning that are carried in words and particularly in technical words. For example, the names of a number of Darwin's great fossil beasts begin with 'Mega'. The dictionary shows this comes from a Greek word meaning 'great' so you know that any creature whose name begins with 'Mega' is a very big one, for example, Megatherium. Compare also Megacycle and Megaton.

Study the list of names used by Darwin on page 126 and their derivations.

5. *English and Science: English and History*

Most of this Appendix so far has been concerned with scientific ways of using English.

Do you think any of this information applies to the kind of writing you do in Science lessons or Science homework?

Does it apply to any of the writing you do in studying History?

Do you, in History, use classification, technical terms, related ideas, and do you have to make theories to explain the facts?

In short, how do you set about answering such questions as—Is it true? What was this used for? What did he really do?

If someone asked you 'Is it likely that there is any foundation of truth in the story of Grendel?' where would you look for an answer?

Some sources of history

Records
The historian compares records by different writers and judges which is most likely to be true.

Objects, Description
The historian looks at things which have been made at the point of time that he is studying. He also reads contemporary descriptions and compares these with the objects.

like speech as you can. Set it out for printing today, which means modern-ising the punctuation as well as the language (see Appendix 3).

17th Century Looter

A person named William Hill, of Tiverton in the county of Devon, who, in the beginning of the Parliament's rebellion, heard that some were demolishing the Earl of Devonshire's chapel, which stood in the church-yard, and were carrying from it what they could. He came thither upon the same wicked design, and found that they had broke to Pieces a Stately Monument made for the Earl and his Countess, and carried away the materials, and the ornaments within, and the Lead at Top, and, upon which, he lamented his misfortune at coming so late, and said, 'Now they have taken away all before I came, and there is nothing left for me.' But looking up, he saw a Bell at the end of it, which they called the Saints Bell. 'Oh!' says he, 'I'll have this.' And getting a ladder he goes up to take it down, and so letting it slip through his hands, the Brim of it cut off his Toes on both Feet, by which means he became a Cripple, and wasting his substance and a small Tenement he had in the cure of his wounds, he became miserably Poor and unfit for Business, went about a-begging upon his Heels with a Crutch and an underhand staff, and so he continued several years, till a gentleman gave him a little Horse, that he might ride further off and beg abroad; and he did for some time, till at last in the Parish of Anstey in this County, he and his Horse were found Dead together in a Ditch. A dismal end of a Sacreligious Person.

From *The Chronicles of Twyford* by F. J. SNELL

APPENDIX 5

The five senses
Proof reading exercise

1. *The five senses*

Everything we know comes to us by way of the five senses.

Discuss this statement: can you think of anything you know that you learned
by any other means?

For study

Look through your accounts of your earliest memories and see how many of
them are about how things looked, or felt or smelt or sounded.

Maps and drawings show the shapes of places and things but they don't
show sounds or smells or tastes.

Words can do this better — though not perfectly.

Here are some things people have said about their sense impressions —
curious but true!

A girl said she saw Sunday as dark blue.

A small girl said she had a yellow pain.

A perfume chemist described a scent as a little flat . . . it needed more
body in the middle tones and less brass at the top.

A man thought low musical notes felt like velvet and high ones like
cutting butter.

Practice exercises

Try writing some short pieces (thumbnail sketches) which express the things
that come to you through your senses.

Suggestions to start you off:

The sounds you hear at night as you lie in bed before you fall asleep.

The sounds you hear in the morning as you lie in bed waiting for someone
to bring you a cup of tea

The feel of the sand as you lie on the beach on a hot day.

2. *Proof reading exercise* (See Appendix 7, page 239)
Re-arrange and punctuate the following as you think it best.

My Brother Bert

Pets are the hobby of my brother bert he used to go to school with a mouse in his shirt his hobby it grew as some hobbies will and grew and grew and grew until oh dont breathe a word pretend you havent heard a simply appalling thing has occurred the very thought makes me iller and iller berts brought home a gigantic gorilla

APPENDIX 6

Anglo-Saxon Poetry
Notes on the history
of the English language
Writing, and reading writing

1. *Anglo-Saxon Poetry*

Seven manuscript copies of *The Anglo-Saxon Chronicle* exist. Five of these are in the British Museum Library in London. Only one copy of *Beowulf* exists and this manuscript is also in the British Museum Library. Old English poetry did not rhyme, but it had a clearly marked rhythm with a pause in the middle of each line; also some of the words in each line began with the same sound.

This made it different from ordinary speech and easier for the 'poem-teller' to remember; and let the listeners know that a tale of great deeds was coming.

e.g.   Him se yldesta   ondswarode
         (Him the eldest   answered)
         Werodes wisa   word-hord onleac
         (Of the troop the leader   word-hoard unlocked)

'The Battle of Maldon' is also a poem, written in this way and probably recited at feasts.

2. *Notes on the history of the English language*

Everything has its history, including, of course, the English language. Here are some events in the history of English:

787 to 994 200 years of Danish invasions and settlement, particularly in the North and East of England. Both English and Danish were spoken and finally a kind of mixed English and Danish language grew up in these parts.

1066 The Norman Conquest. For 300 years the official language was French, so many people had to speak both languages.

1362 English was made the official language of the law courts but by this time it had become a mixture of French and English, entirely

228

coming of p

had spelled as words *sounaeu* ⸺ ⸺

changed much less because the language of books existeu as a ⸺ of standard.

3. *Writing, and reading writing*

Writing is one thing, and reading what someone else has written is another and very different thing. You have to be able to read it, *and* to understand it.

When people write, they have their mental eye on their memories or their ideas – on the pursuit and capture of their thoughts – and they let their pens do the best they can to get all this down without much attention, because it is an interruption to writing to have to stop and decide how to spell a word. When the story or the ideas have been roughly trapped in words, then is the time to go back and see how your pen has managed its job, correct the spelling, put in some punctuation marks, and see that the handwriting is readable. Then too, a writer reads his own story (or poem or report) to see if it says what he meant.

But reading someone else's writing is more difficult than reading your own, because the only clue you have to what the writer meant is what the words on the page say.

Each member of a school class was asked to read a story (or poem) by another member of the class and to write a comment on it. Here are some of the things the children wrote about each other's work.

1. Quite humorous. The writing is good and so is the spelling. You started off well with a good setting for the story.

2. Try not to put things down twice!

3. It is too short and I cannot read it.

4. Good, but too many sentences containing lists.

5. Boring! I am sure it was exciting for you but it does not make good reading.

6. Very good. Make it a bit neater. Sounds more like an adult's poem. [By a second reader:] I don't agree that it's like an adult's poem. It is a good poem but I couldn't read it very well.

7. Rather untidy. A bit jerky; try to join up your sentences. Too much like a newspaper report. Don't go on to the next page with the same word.

8. Too short. You don't write anything about your feelings.

9. Short, but I get a full impression of a November afternoon. Good.

10. What is it all about? I can't read it.

These are interesting remarks, but most of the children found the handwriting difficult to read. *Try this for yourselves — and when revising your work remember the poor reader.*
Consider this account of a camping holiday. If you struggle through it, it is rather interesting and it has miniature illustrations in the text so that they almost look as if they were part of the writing system.
Try reading it aloud, which is a good test of the legibility of handwriting.

in ~~I and~~ Brian well and Roger in other one ~~between~~ between Then and I ~~took~~ Vic's kit bag. ~~so~~

We found a nice ~~spot~~ and Vick ~~pitched~~ put the tents up one ~~be~~ besige ~~the~~ the ~~other~~ like this Roger and ~~den~~ sleep in the first tent and Vic ~~&~~ Brian and I sleep in the big tent and he put the store tent like this agast a tree ~~of~~ that night ~~to~~ Len ~~and~~ Roger went off ~~to sleep~~ strait away but we didnt we were awake all the night having fun telling jokes and ~~so~~ on.

Next morning Roger and ~~I~~ ~~took~~ Len moved their tent ~~so~~ it looked like this

APPENDIX 7

Plays and fables
Moods and tenses
Instructions, reports, commentary
English and Science
How to correct your own written work

1. *Plays and fables*

Characters:

Herr Biedermann:	A wealthy Swiss gentleman
Anna:	A maid
Schmitz:	A stranger

The Fire Raisers

Anna turns to go, and sees that the stranger has just entered: An athlete, his clothes are reminiscent both of a jail and of a circus, his arms are tattooed, and he wears leather straps round his wrists. Anna creeps out. The stranger waits till Biedermann has sipped his wine and looks round.

Schmitz: Good evening.

> *Biedermann drops his cigar with astonishment.*

Your cigar, Herr Biedermann –

> *He picks up the cigar and gives it to Biedermann.*

Biedermann: I say –

Schmitz: Good Evening!

Biedermann: What's the meaning of this? I expressly told the maid you were to wait out in the hall. What possessed you ... I mean ... without knocking ...

Schmitz: My name is Schmitz.

Biedermann: Without knocking.

Schmitz: Joseph Schmitz.

232

Schmitz: A wrestler by trade.

Biedermann: A wrestler?

Schmitz: A heavy-weight.

Biedermann: I see.

Schmitz: That's to say, I was.

Biedermann: And now?

Schmitz: I'm out of work.

Pause.

Don't worry, Herr Biedermann, I'm not looking for work.
On the contrary. I'm fed up with wrestling . . . I only came
in because it's raining so hard outside.

Pause.

It's warmer in here.

Pause.

I hope I'm not disturbing you –

Pause.

Biedermann: Do you smoke?

He offers cigars.

Schmitz: It's terrible to be as big as I am, Herr Biedermann. Everyone's afraid of me. . . .

Biedermann gives him a light.

Thanks.

They stand smoking.

Q

Biedermann: To come to the point, what do you want?

Schmitz: My name is Schmitz.

Biedermann: So you said, well, how do you do?

Schmitz: I'm homeless.

> *He holds the cigar under his nose and savours the aroma.*

I'm homeless.

Biedermann: Would you like – a slice of bread?

Schmitz: If that's all you've got. . . .

Biedermann: Or a glass of wine?

Schmitz: Bread and wine. . . . But only if I'm not disturbing you, Herr Biedermann, only if I'm not disturbing you!

> *Biedermann goes to the door.*

Biedermann: Anna!

> *Biedermann comes back.*

From *The Fire Raisers* by M AX F RISCH

A sinister start. Finish the scene perhaps.

A play script has to contain:

1. *The words the actors speak*
2. *Instructions for some of their actions*, though actors are left free to improvise (make up) most of their movements as they think fit.
3. In modern plays, some instructions about what the characters are like and what they are to wear. In old plays, these last instructions were omitted. Shakespeare, for instance, has very few *stage directions*, i.e., instructions for the actors.

Study the way this scene from *The Fire Raisers* is set out. Notice there is nothing in the text except *the words* the characters are to speak, printed opposite their names, and the *stage directions* (instructions as to the movements they *must* make, whatever other ones they perform in addition to these.)

Read the fable on page 187 'The Wolf Who Went Places' by James Thurber.

A fable is a story with a moral; often the characters in fables are animals who behave and speak like human beings.

Rewrite this story as a ...

2. *Moods and tenses*

Mood means *mode* or *way* of doing something.

Tense comes from the French 'le temps' = time.

Verbs have many different forms.

Tenses

If you want to say that you will be doing something soon or a long time ahead you use the *future tense*.

for example, *I shall be ready* in a few minutes, or

   He will find out soon.

If you want to say what is happening now, you use the *present tense*.

for example, *I am ready*.

   I am doing my homework.

If you want to report what has happened, you use a *past tense* (there are a lot of these).

for example, *I was ready*.

   I have done my homework.

   I found half-a-crown.

Moods (Mode — manner, way of doing something)

As well as showing whether something happened in the past, is happening now, or will happen in the future, verbs say something about the *manner* or way in which things are done.

NOTES ABOUT AUTHORS

APOLLONIUS OF RHODES: poet, teacher and director of the great library at Alexandria. He was writing about 250 B.C. The story given here is taken from his *Argonautica*, the full account of Jason's search for the Golden Fleece.

VALERIE AVERY began her book *London Morning* while she was still at school. She went to college and finished the book when she came back as an English teacher at her comprehensive school. She is now married and lives in South London.

W. H. BARRETT made two collections of the stories told to him by the old people living in the Fen district of East Anglia: *Tales from the Fens*, and *More Tales from the Fens*. WILLIAM KEMP and DUSTY MILLER told him the two stories quoted in this book.

BERTOLT BRECHT: a German playwright and poet. He went to America when the Nazis came to power but returned to East Berlin after the War. Most of his plays and poems have been translated and *The Caucasian Chalk Circle*, *The Life of Galileo*, *Mother Courage* and *The Good Woman of Setzuan* are frequently performed in England

RACHEL CARSON: an American marine biologist. Her writing includes *The Sea around Us*, *The Edge of the Sea*, and *Under the Sea Wind*; this last is about the birds and other creatures of the American coasts.

JOYCE CARY has written many novels. *A House of Children* is an autobiographical novel about his childhood in Ireland. *Charlie is My Darling* is about London children evacuated to the country during the bombing raids of 1940.

CHARLES CAUSLEY is an English poet who writes and teaches in the Cornish town of Launceston.

PADRAIC COLUM: an Irish poet writing to-day. He made the collection *Myths of the World* from which the story of Ma-ui is taken.

CHARLES DARWIN went as a naturalist on a naval surveying expedition to South America and adjacent islands. The voyage lasted 5 years and he recorded his observations on natural history and geology in his journal – *The Voyage of the Beagle 1837*. In 1859 he published his *Origin of Species* and in 1871 *The Descent of Man*.

SIR ARTHUR CONAN DOYLE created the character of Sherlock Holmes; he also wrote historical novels (*White Company*) and *The Lost World* which is a forerunner of science fiction.

JEAN DE JOINVILLE: A French ... by King Louis IX of France to fight the seventh cru... Life of King Louis to a scribe. It has been translated from mediaeval French into modern English.

FRANZ KAFKA was a Czech writer who died in 1924. His best known books are *The Trial* and *The Castle*.

DAVID LACK is a distinguished ornithologist. His book *The Life of the Robin* is based on what he found out about the local robins when he was teaching at Dartington Hall School in South Devon.

SEAN O'CASEY: An Irish playwright who wrote an autobiography about growing up as a poor boy in Dublin, getting involved in revolutionary activities, and becoming a writer.

SYLVIA PLATH: an American poetess who married an English poet (Ted Hughes). She died in 1963.

SAKI: the pen name of H. H. Munro. He wrote many short stories; most of them are politely unkind about unkind people. He was killed in action in the First World War.

IAN SERRAILLIER: a poet and story writer. He made the translation into poetry of part of the Anglo-Saxon poem *Beowulf* and called it *Beowulf the Warrior*.

JAMES THURBER: American writer and artist. He began to write when he was 10 and to draw when he was 14. He described his stories as 'mainly humorous but with a few kind-of-sad-ones'. His drawings are like this too. He died in 1961.

LEO TOLSTOY: Russian novelist. His most famous books are *War and Peace* and *Anna Karenina. My Elder Brother* came from his autobiographical story called *Childhood, Boyhood, Youth* which was published in 1852 when he was 24.

MONIQUE WITTIG is a French novelist writing to-day. *The Attackers* comes from a story about some girls growing up and going to school at a convent.

YEVGENY YEVTUSHENKO: a young Russian who was not sure whether he was going to become a poet or a sports journalist. His first poem was published in a football paper. He is now an established Soviet poet. He has also written his auto-biography.

ACKNOWLEDGEMENTS

The author would like to thank the following copyright holders for permission to use extracts from their books.

Apollonius of Rhodes: 'The Argonauts escape with the Golden Fleece and the Princess' from *The Voyage of the Argo*. Trans. E. V. Rieu. Reprinted by permission of Penguin Books Ltd.

Valerie Avery: 'Gran' and 'Grandad' from *London Morning*. Reprinted by permission of William Kimber & Co. Ltd.

W. H. Barrett: 'Bone Meal in the Flour' and 'Witches at Hallowe'en' from *More Tales from the Fens*. Ed. Enid Porter. Reprinted by permission of Routledge & Kegan Paul Ltd.

Bertolt Brecht: 'Questions of a Studious Working Man' from *Tales from the Calendar*. Trans. M. Hamburger. Reprinted by permission of Methuen & Co. Ltd.

Rachel Carson: 'The Secret Life of the Beaches' from *The Edge of the Sea* (Mac-Gibbon & Kee Ltd.). Reprinted by permission of Marie Rodell, Literary Trustee, and Houghton, Mifflin & Co. of Boston.

Joyce Cary: 'The Cave at Shell Port' from *A House of Children*. Reprinted by permission of Michael Joseph Ltd.

Charles Causley: 'Nursery Rhyme of Innocence and Experience' from *Union Street* (Rupert Hart-Davis). Reprinted by permission of David Higham Associates Ltd.

Padraic Colum: 'How Ma-ui strove to win Immortality for all Creatures' from *Myths of the World* (Crowell, Collier and Macmillan Inc.).

Charles Darwin: 'Darwin finds the Fossil Bones of Prehistoric Monsters' from *The Voyage of the Beagle 1831–36* (Bantam Books Edition 1958).

Sir Arthur Conan Doyle: *The Lost World*. Reprinted by permission of John Murray Ltd. and the Trustees of the Estate of Sir Arthur Conan Doyle.

Max Frisch: *The Fire Raisers* translated by Michael Bullock. Reprinted by permission of Methuen & Co. Ltd.

R. K. Gordon: *The Battle of Maldon* (Everyman's Library edition). Reprinted by permission of J. M. Dent & Sons Ltd.

John Holmes: *A Map of my Country*. Reprinted by permission of Mrs. Doris Holmes.

Miroslav Holub: 'A Boy's Head', 'The Door', Fairy Tale' and 'A History Lesson' from *Selected Poems* trans. by Ian Milner and George Theiner. Reprinted by permission of Penguin Books Ltd.

Ted Hughes: 'My Brother Bert' from *Meet My Folks!* Reprinted by permission of Faber & Faber Ltd.

Mrs. Humphries from the *Padstow Echo*.

N. H. Joy: *How to Know British Birds*. Reprinted by permission of H. F. & G. Witherby Ltd.

Franz Kafka: *Metamorphosis*. Reprinted by permission of Martin Secker & Warburg Ltd. and Schocken Books Ltd.

Richard Kell: *Pigeons*. Reprinted by permission of Mr. R. Kell.

David Lack: *The Life of the Robin*. Reprinted by permission of Mr. D. Lack.

Oxford University Press.

James Thurber: 'The Wolf who went places' from *Vintage Thurber* by James Thurber, copyright © 1963 Hamish Hamilton, London, and copyright © 1956 James Thurber from *Further Fables for our Time* published by Simon & Schuster, New York. Originally printed in the *New Yorker*.

Leo Tolstoy: 'My Elder Brother' from *Childhood, Boyhood, Youth*. Reprinted by permission of Penguin Books Ltd.

U.H.E.R. 800: 'Threading the Tape' from Operating Instructions.

Constance Whyte: *More than a Legend*. Reprinted by permission of Hamish Hamilton Ltd.

Monique Wittig: 'The Attackers' from *The Opoponax*. Reprinted by permission of Peter Owen and Simon & Schuster Inc. English translation © 1966 by Simon & Schuster Inc.

Yevgeny Yevtushenko: *On a Bicycle*. Reprinted by permission of Penguin Books Ltd.

Graham, M.C.E., Kenneth, Anna, Linda, Peter, John, June, Anthony, Ian, Pat, Lindsay, Margaret, Marilyn, Peggy, Henry, Barry, Simon, George, Brian, Lorraine for permission to reprint their poems and prose pieces.

The author would also like to thank the many friends who have contributed writing done by their pupils and who have tried out some of the suggestions in this book. Thanks are due also to members of the London Association for the Teaching of English and to colleagues in the English Department at the London Institute of Education. The ideas about English teaching which are embodied in the book are to a large extent the product of discussions and work together over a long period.

The Publishers would like to thank the following for permission to reproduce photographs:

British Museum: page 142, 175; Jane Gate: 8, 12, 16, 41, 50, 55, 62, 63, 66 top, 67, 68, 69, 70, 73, 76, 86, 89, 92, 95, 102, 120, 130, 153, 160, 166, 170, 186 and the cover; Henry Grant: 61, 71, 74, 146, 157, 191, 196, 201, 227; London Express News and Feature Service: 123; Mansell Collection: 18; Roger Mayne: 36, 66 bottom, 72, 74, 85; Universitetets Oldsaksamling, Oslo: 173; Pierpont Morgan Library, New York: 180; T. W. Snow: 31; D. C. Smith: 207; John Massey Stewart: 134.

INDEX OF AUTHORS

INDEX